AF356493

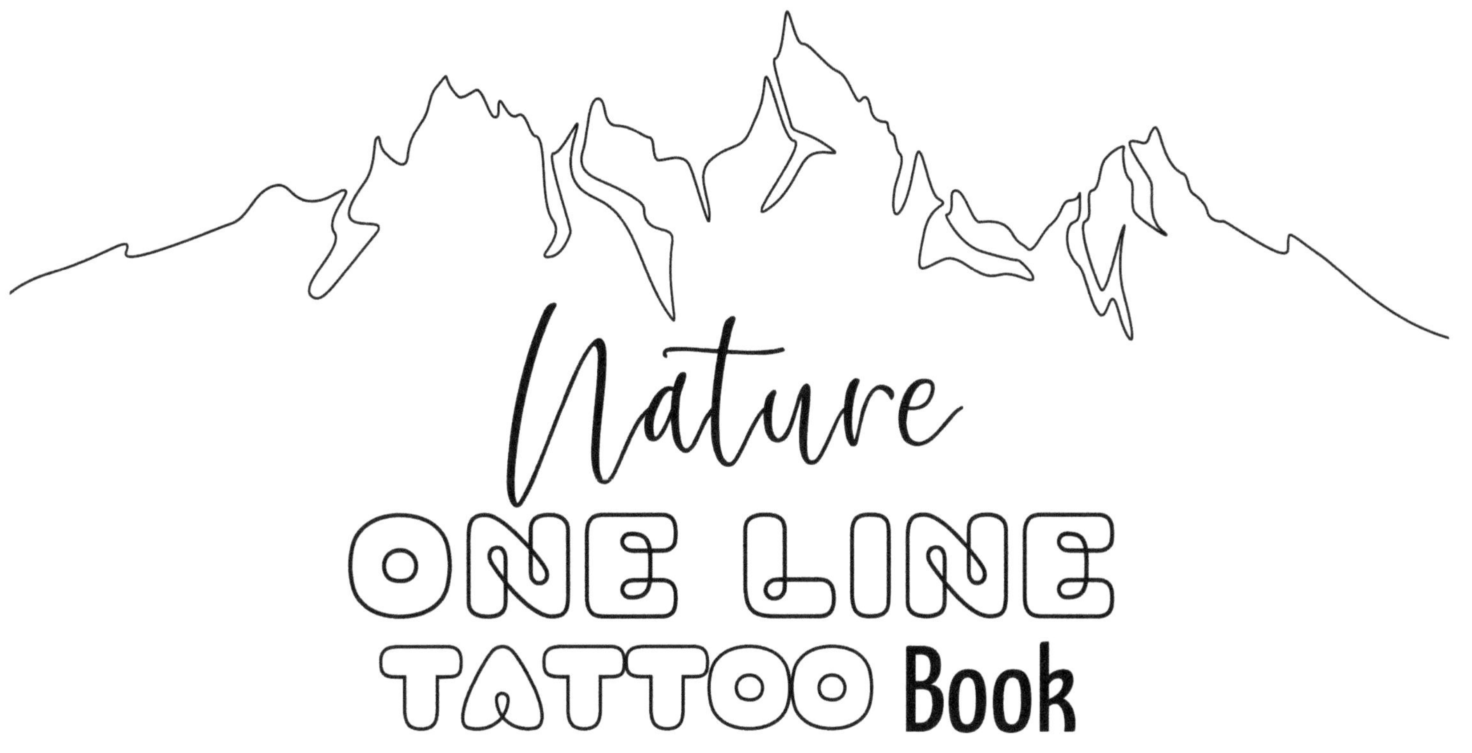

Nature
ONE LINE
TATTOO Book

over 800 tattoo designs

for minimal lovers

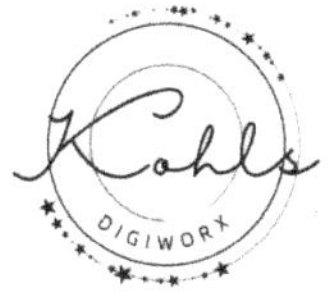

This tattoo template book offers a large selection of small, minimal and fine nature tattoo designs that are perfect for Fine Line, One Line, and the Single Needle technique.

One of the most important reasons for choosing a small tattoo is probably the beginner friendliness. These small designs are excellent, especially for people who have not yet had any tattooing experience and would like to familiarize themselves with the art of tattooing. Work and social environment often play a role in choosing a fine line tattoo, which can be worn discreetly in any walk of life or professional situation. They are certainly an eye-catcher.

After all, the mini tattoos offer decisive advantages:

Small tattoos and the duration:
The tattooing process does not take long and the costs are reasonable.

Small tattoos and the pain:
The pain factor also often plays a minor role with a small and fine motif, and should you ever become dissatisfied with your decision, the tattoos can easily be covered or removed by laser.

Small tattoos as a reminder:
Small tattoos are also so popular because they offer a good and subtle way to capture memories, for example of a vacation, a good friend, or a dramatic life event.

In recent years, several styles have been established that are explicitly intended for tattooing small designs or are at least well suited for this.

Fine Line:
It is probably the most common style when it comes to mini tattoos and it is usually the best for it. The Fine Line style is self-explanatory.The tattoo artist uses a needle that is as fine or small as possible for the entire subject. Shades and too many details are often avoided and the tattoos are mainly defined by minimalism and very delicate lines.

One Line:
The focus here is less on which needles are used and more on the fact that only one needle size is used. This type of tattoo can be done in a very fine way as well as with thicker lines. Since the tattoo consists of only one continuous line, there is no shading in this style either and the details are usually rather marginal.

Single Needle:
With a single needle, the tattoo artist uses the smallest possible needle size for the entire design. Accordingly, it is a combination of the first two styles mentioned. However, in contrast to the Fine Line, the Single Needle style is not exclusively used for small tattoos. It is also used for large designs. But unlike Fine Line and One Line, with this style, far more details and shades are possible and even important because the more contrast a single-needle tattoo has, the better it ultimately comes into its own.

Whatever technique you choose, this book provides 837 tattoo ideas that will help you find a trendy, small and nature inspired motif to make your dream tattoo come true.

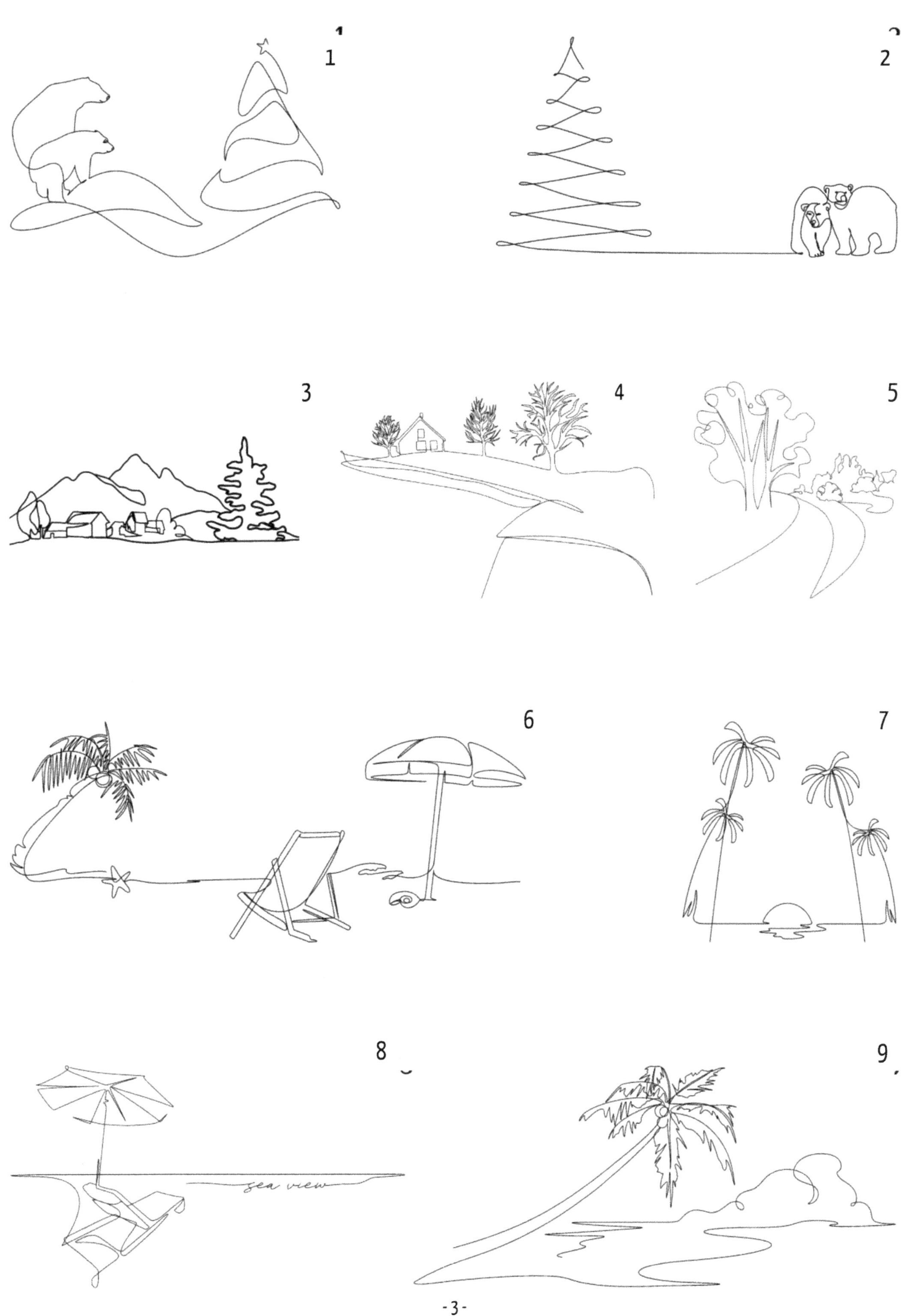

1
2
3
4
5
6
7
8
sea view
9

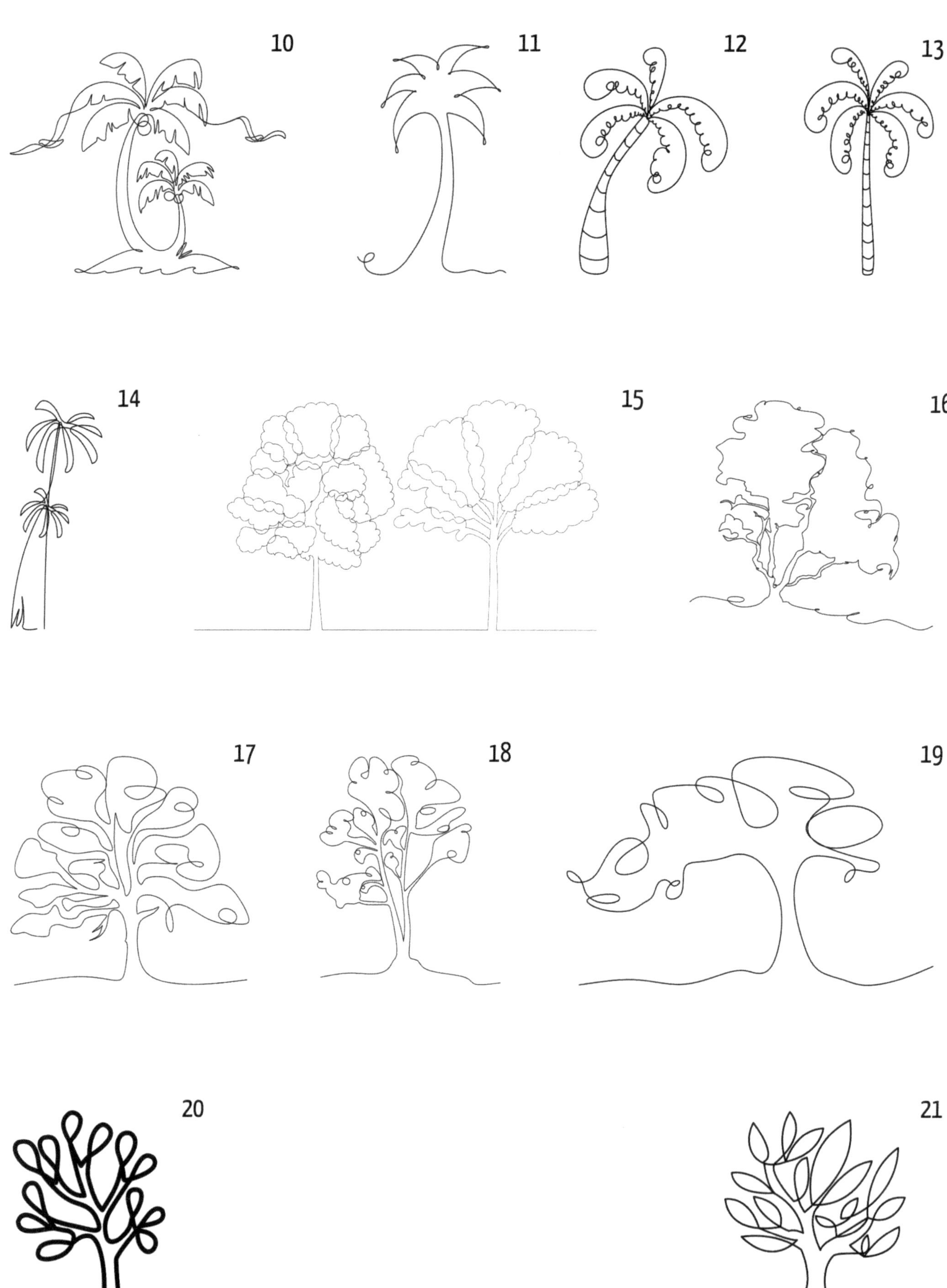

10
11
12
13
14
15
16
17
18
19
20
21

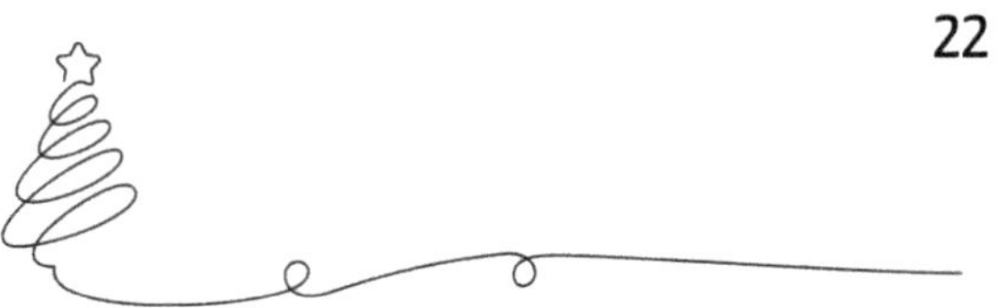

22

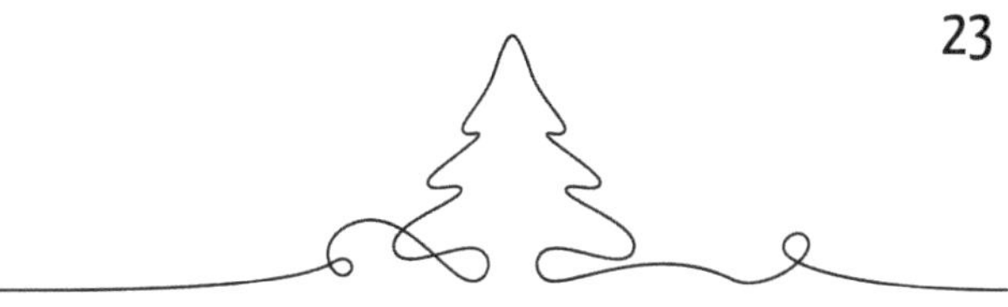

23

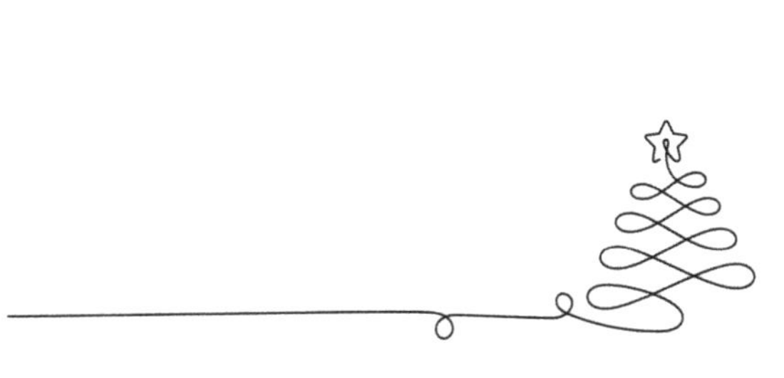

23

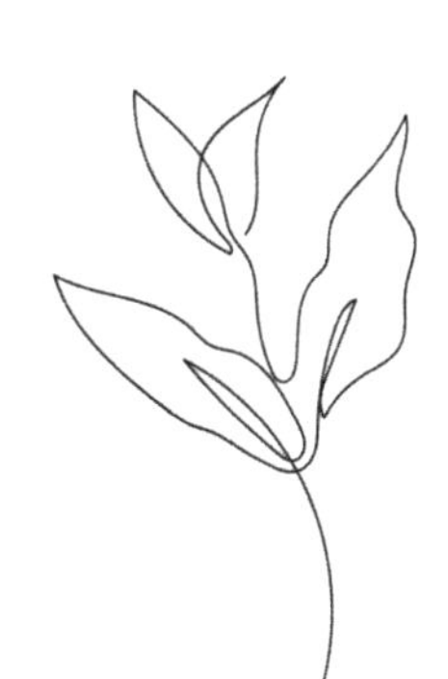

24

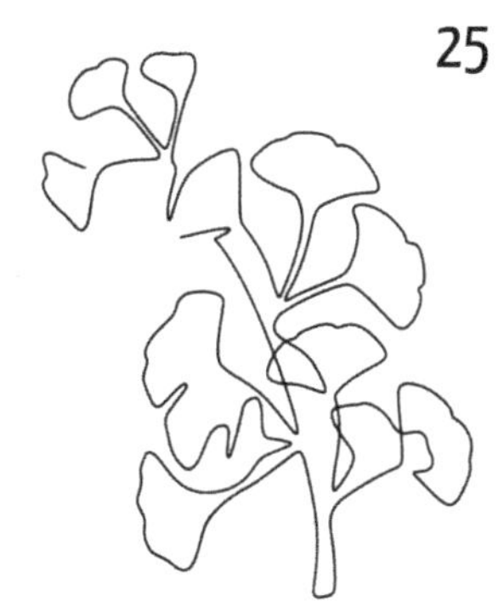

25

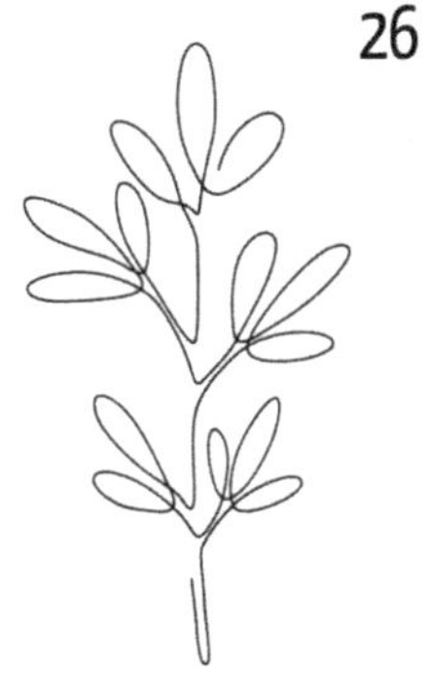

26

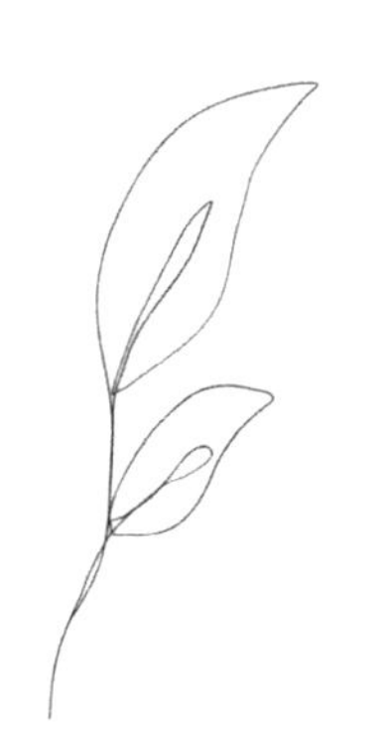

27

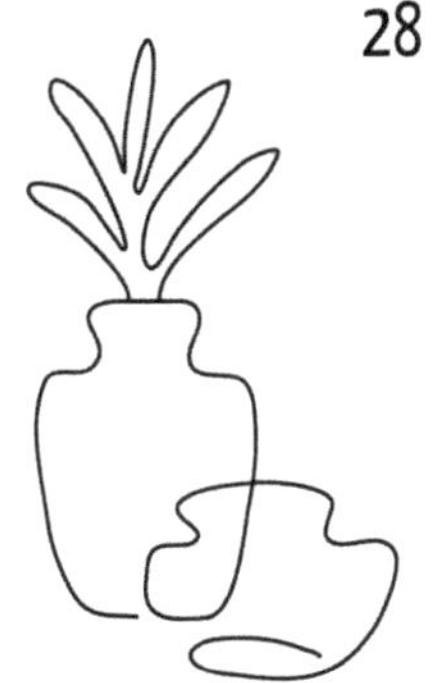

28

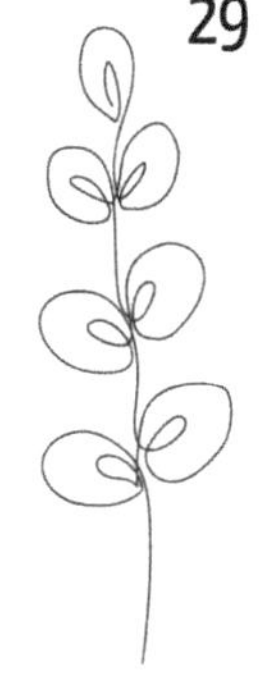

29

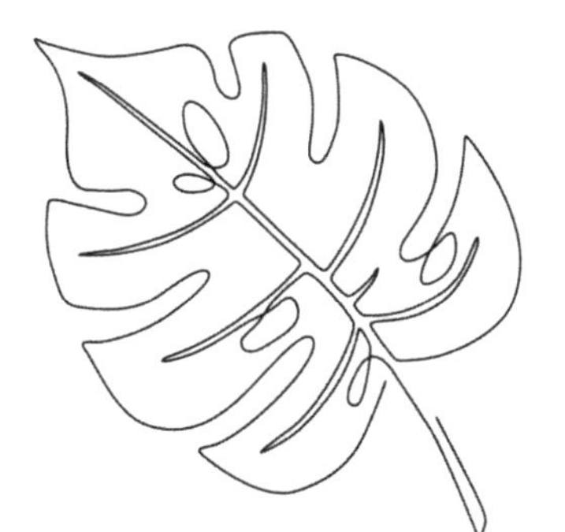

30

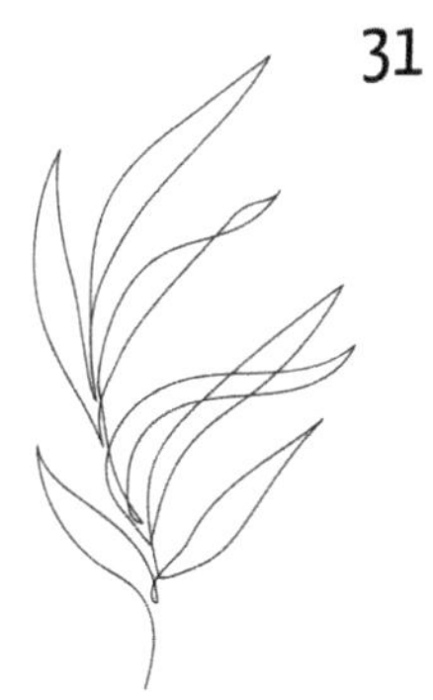

31

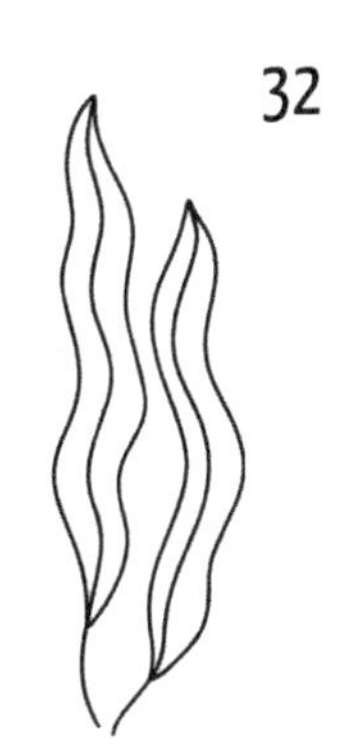

32

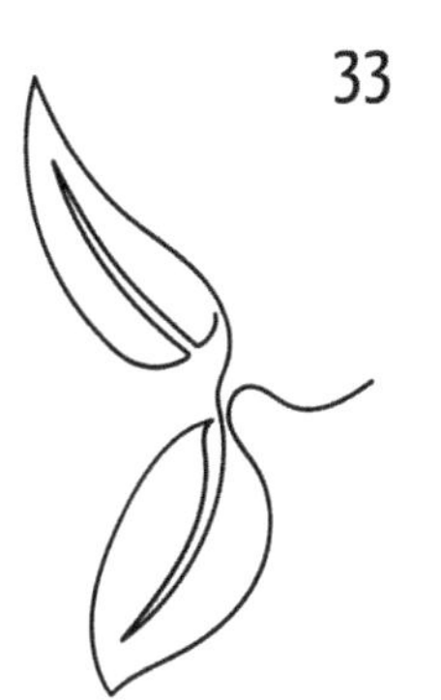

33

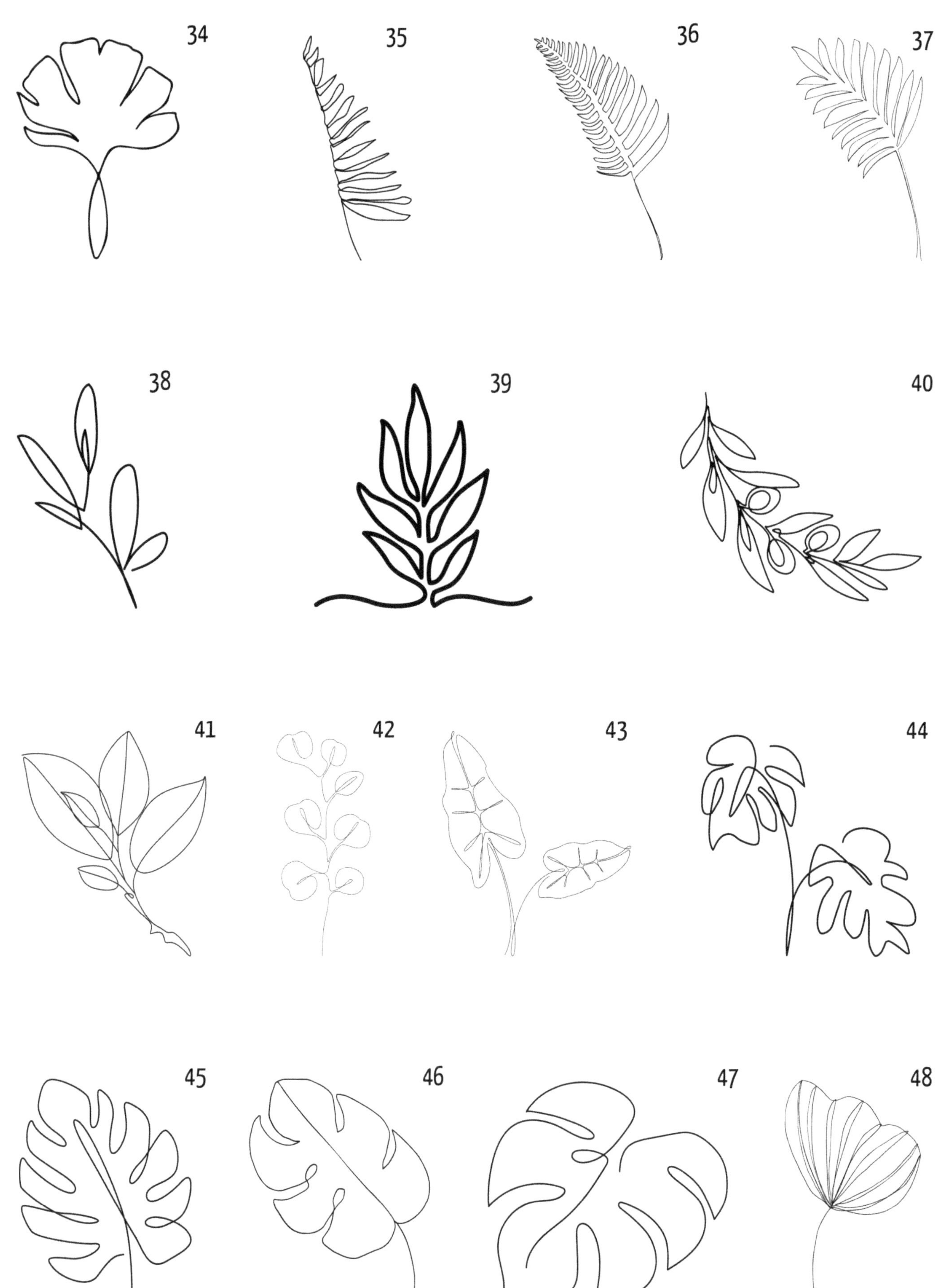

34
35
36
37
38
39
40
41
42
43
44
45
46
47
48

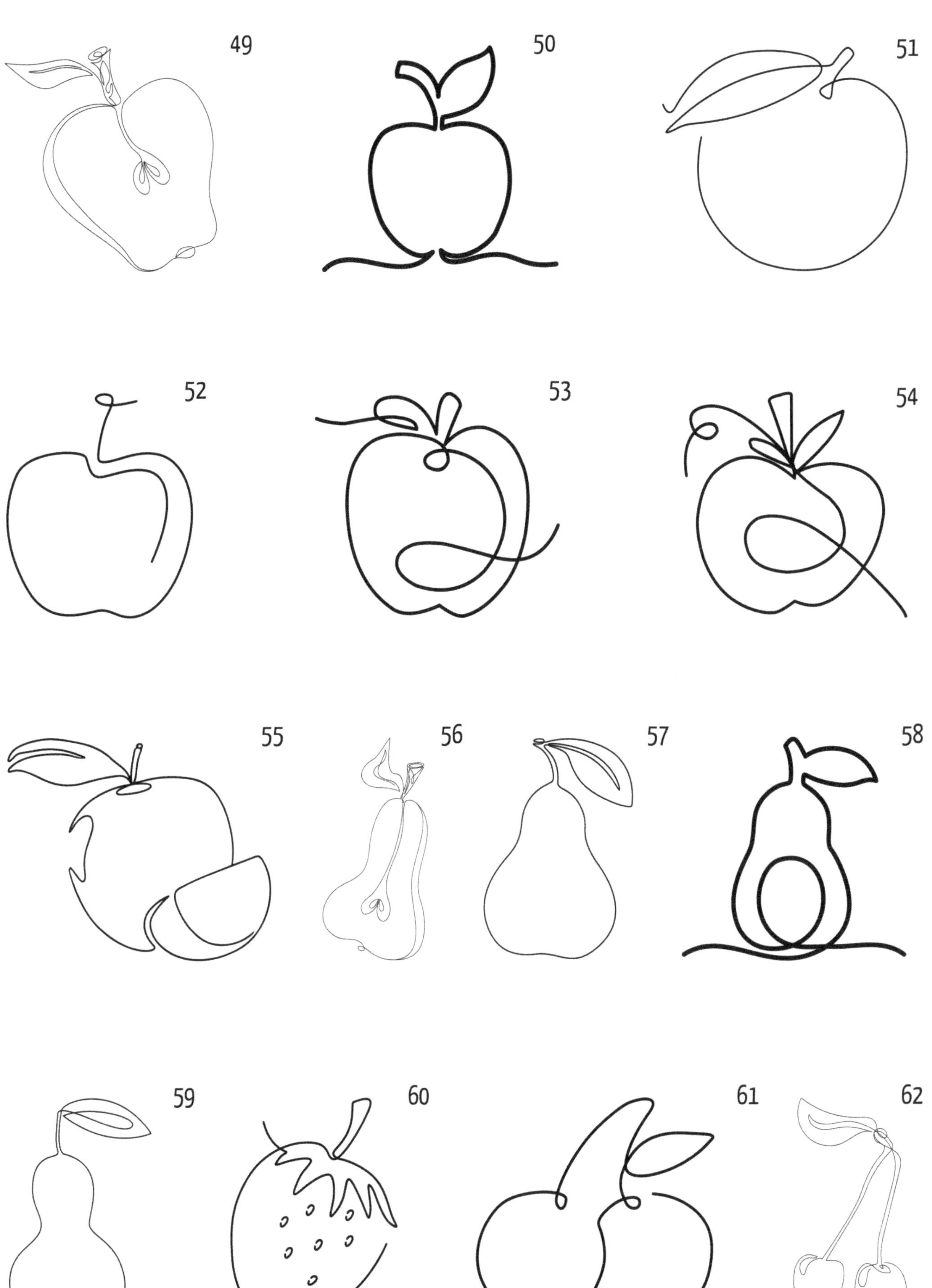

49
50
51
52
53
54
55
56
57
58
59
60
61
62

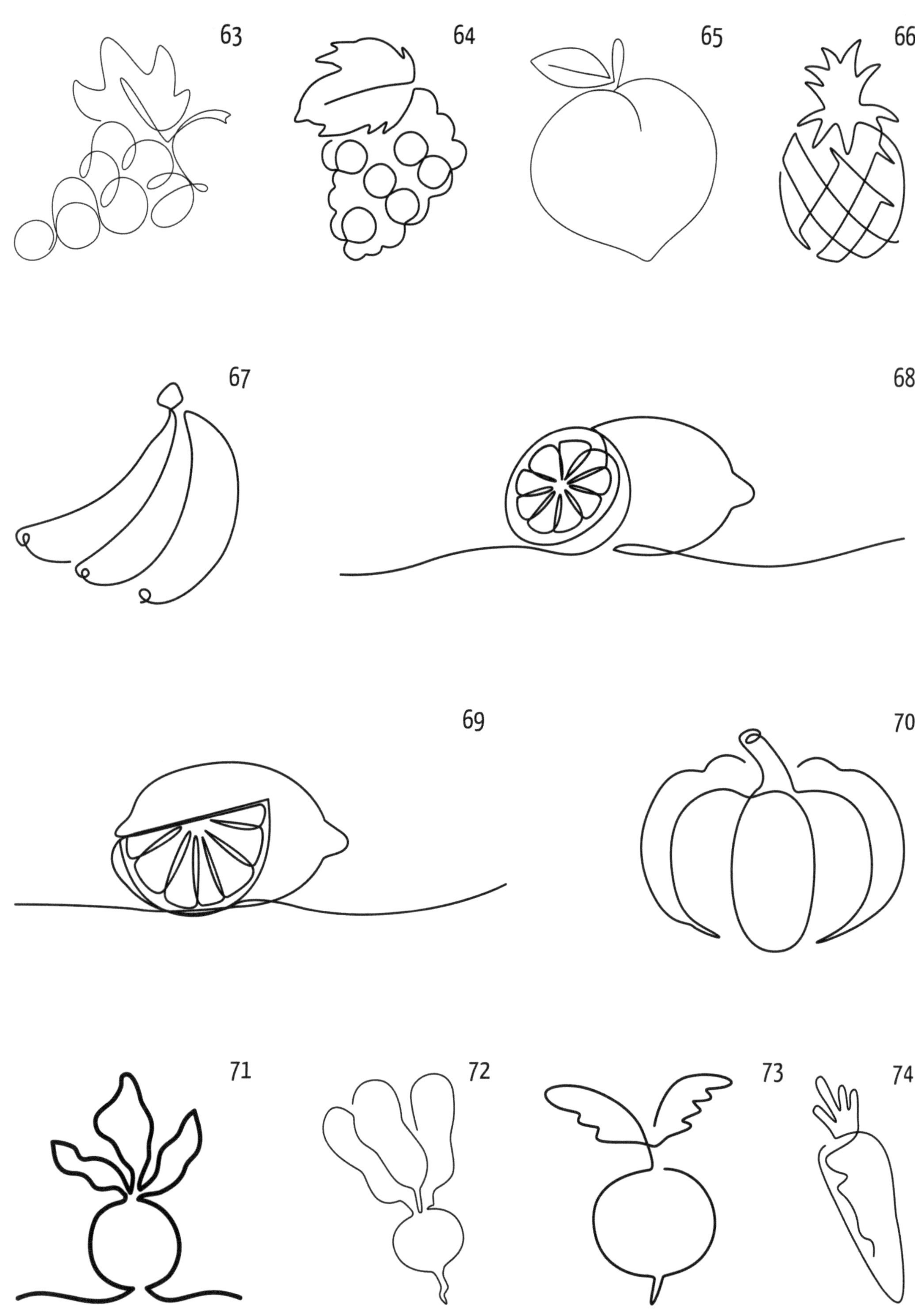

63
64
65
66
67
68
69
70
71
72
73
74

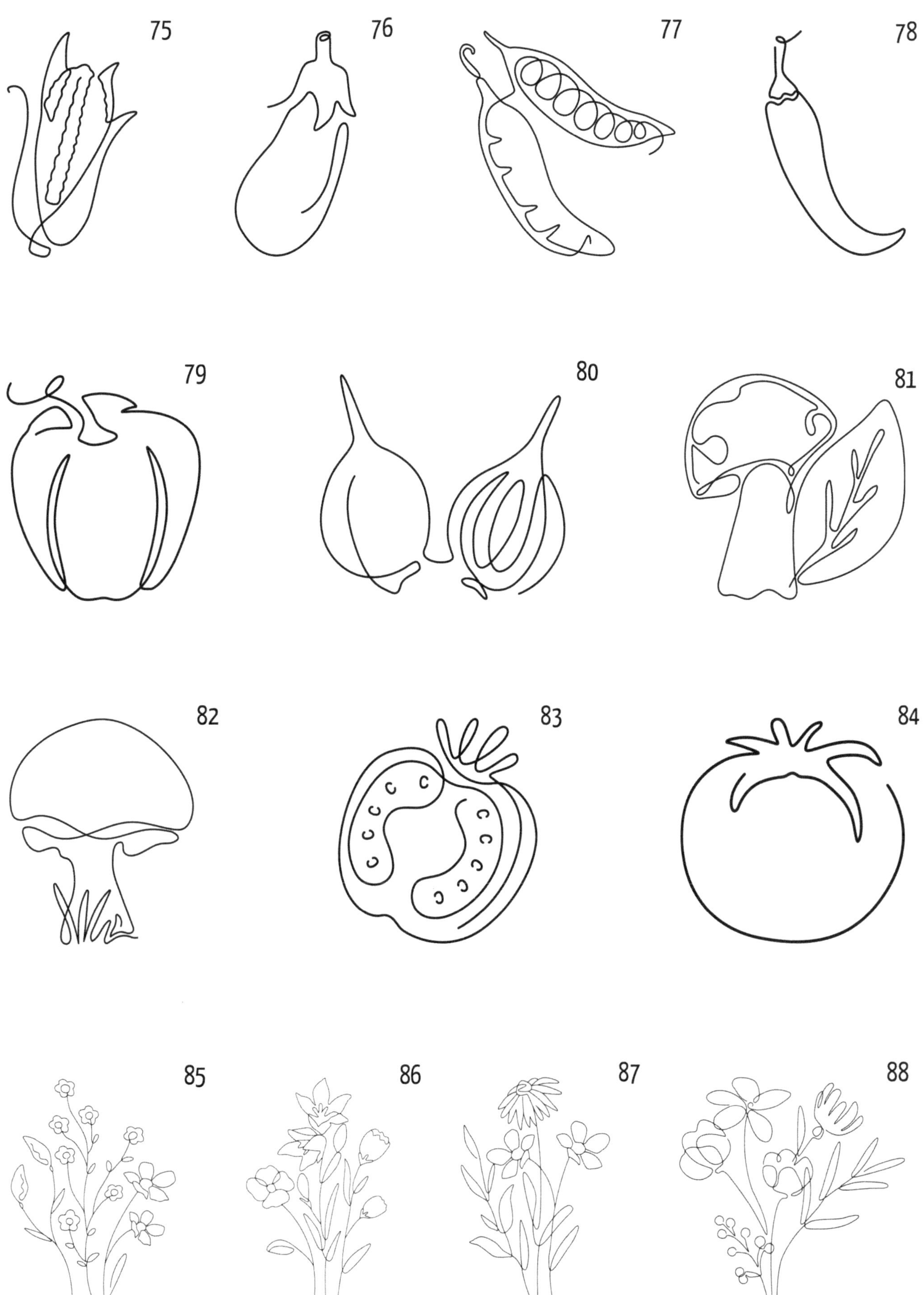

75
76
77
78
79
80
81
82
83
84
85
86
87
88

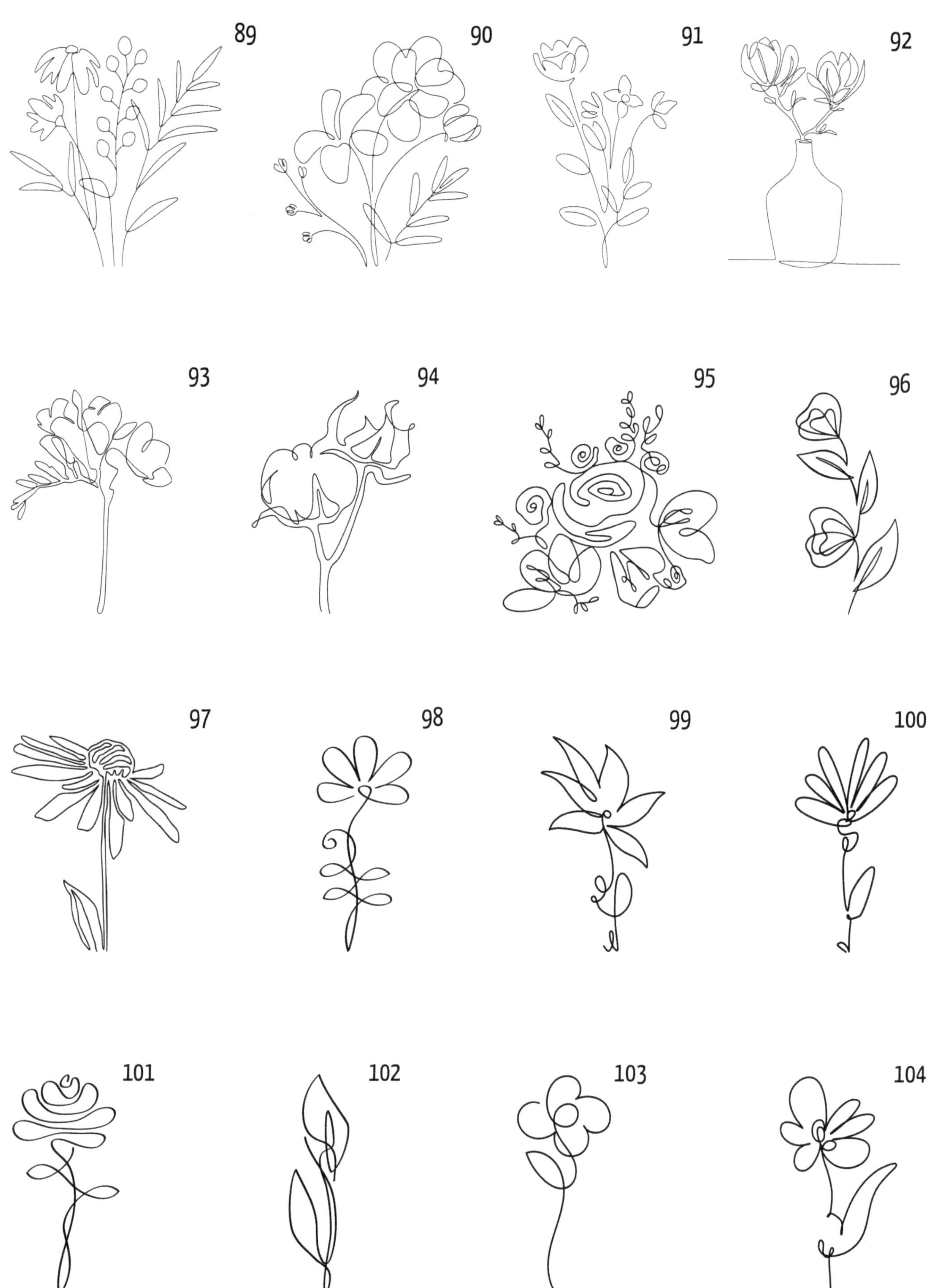

89
90
91
92
93
94
95
96
97
98
99
100
101
102
103
104

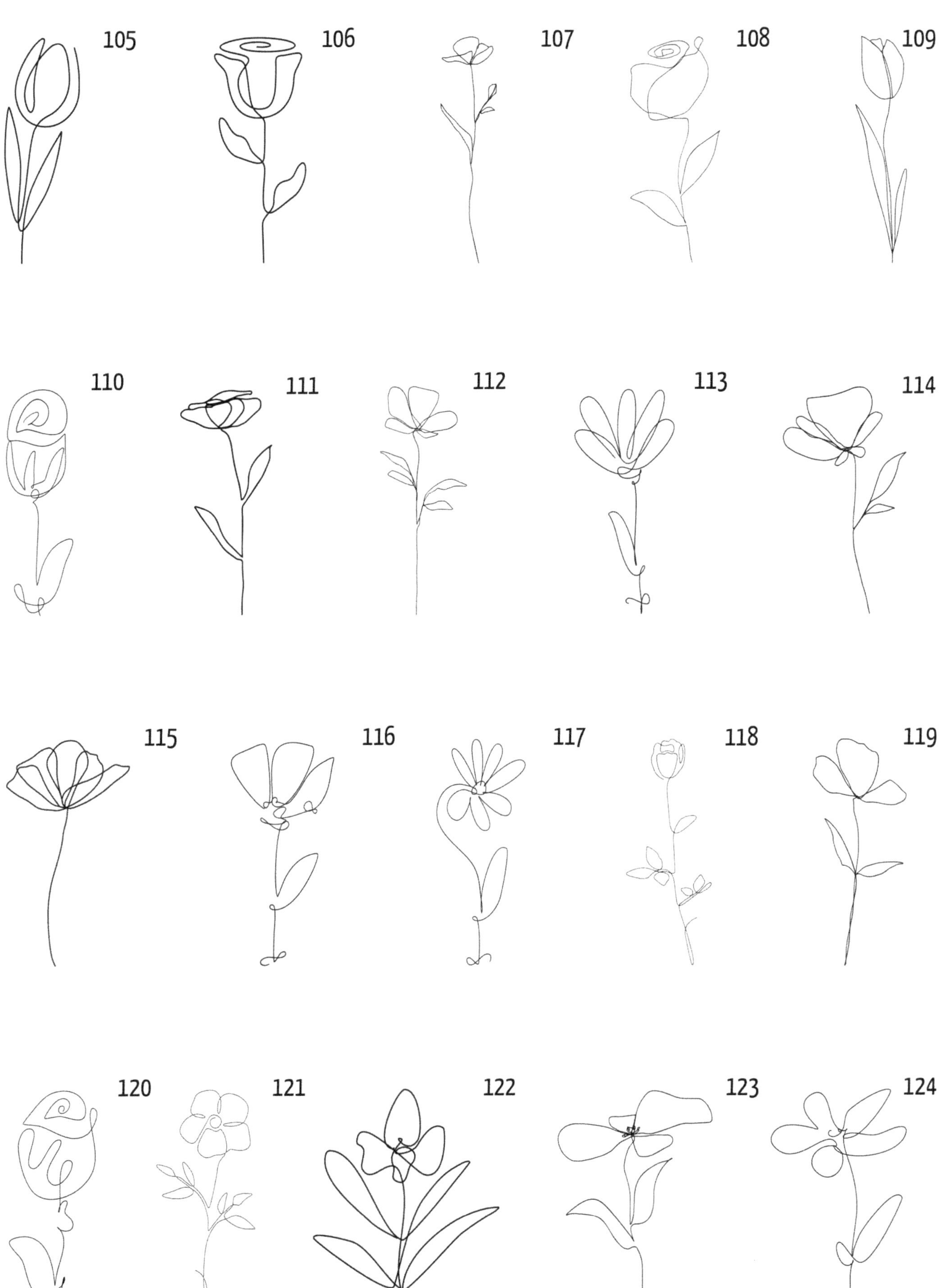

105
106
107
108
109
110
111
112
113
114
115
116
117
118
119
120
121
122
123
124

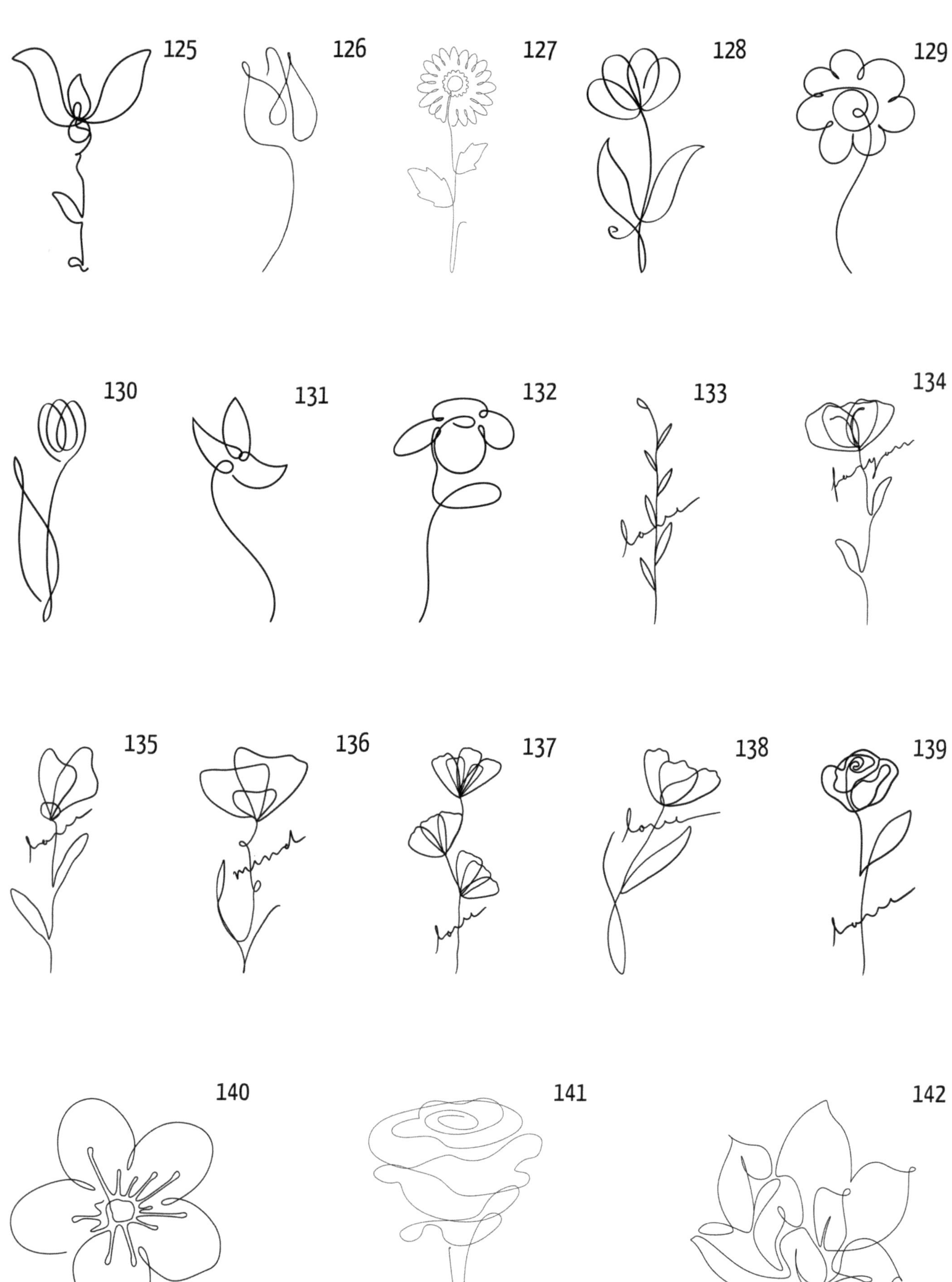

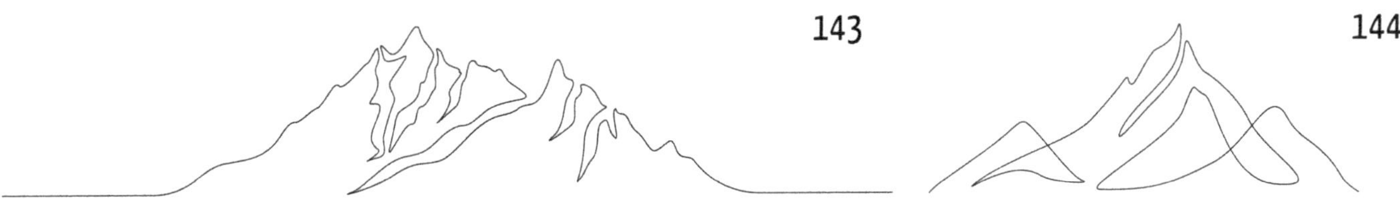

143

144

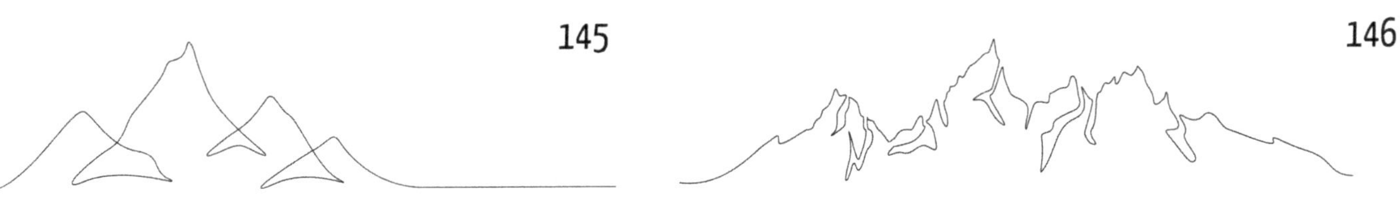

145

146

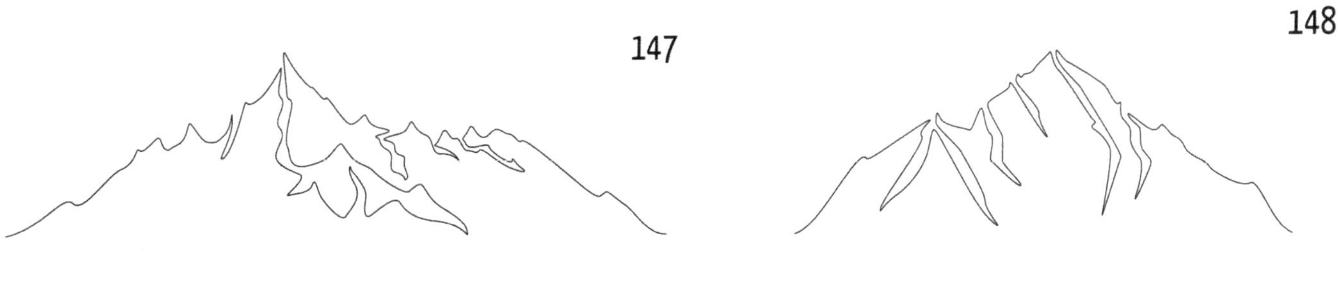

147

148

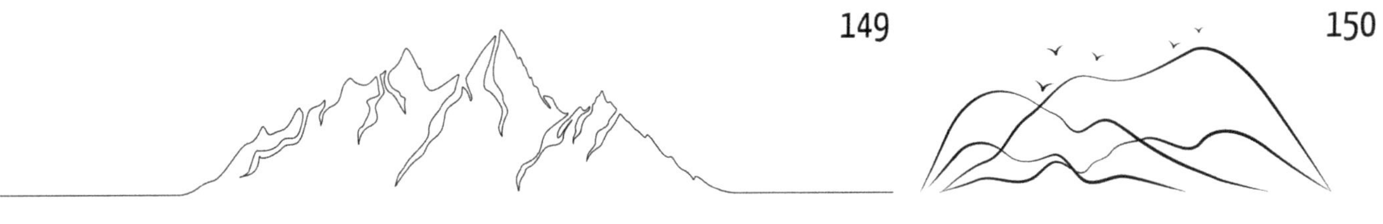

149

150

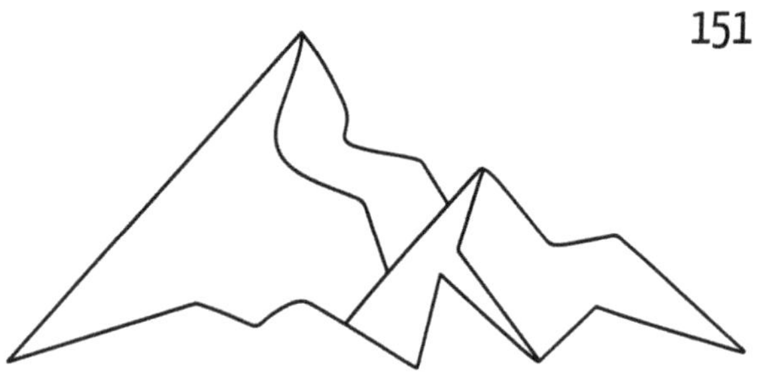

151

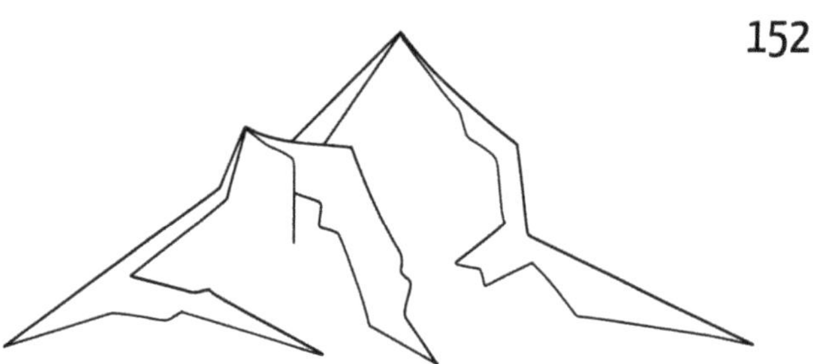

152

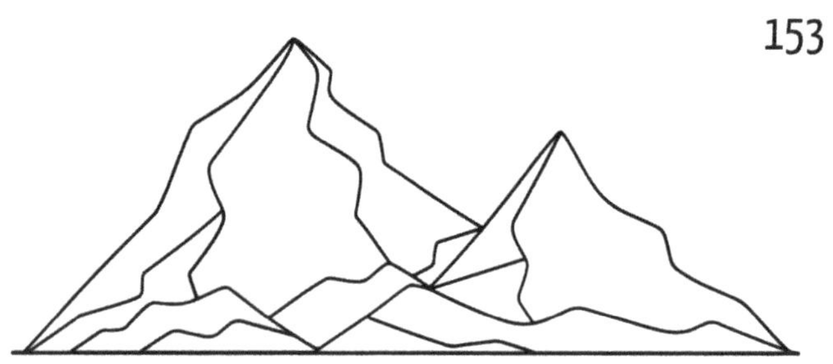

153

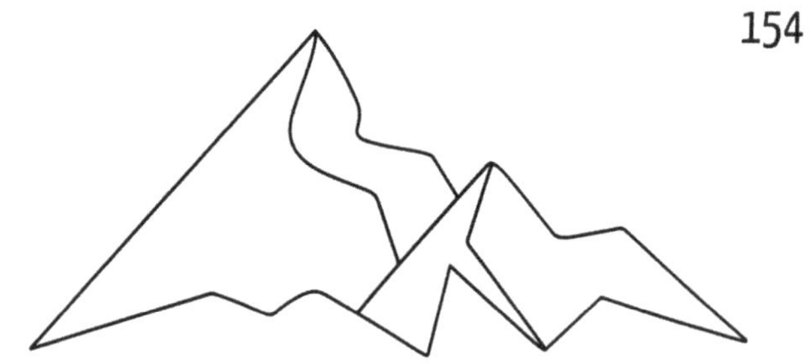

154

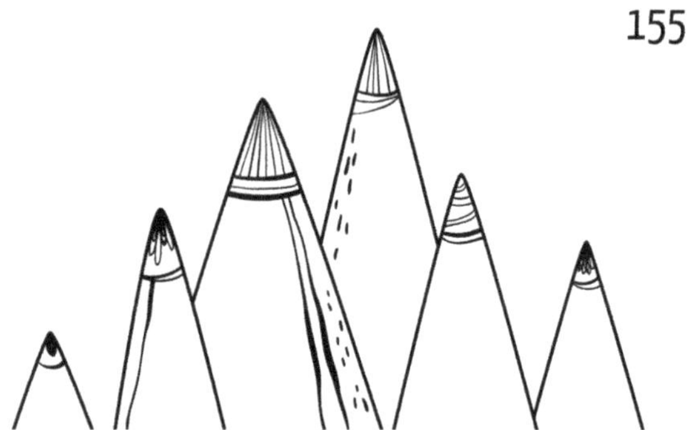

155

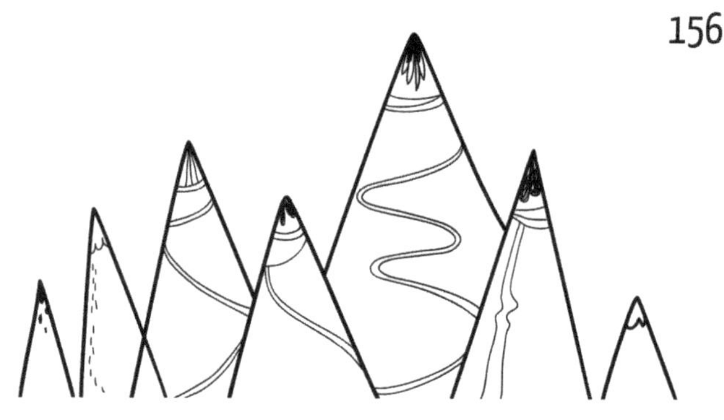

156

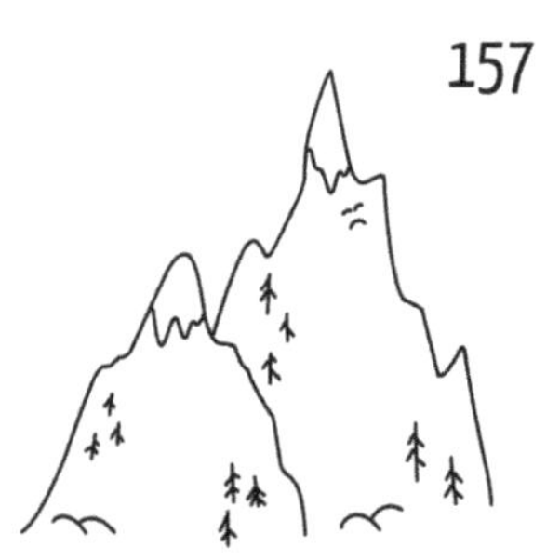

157

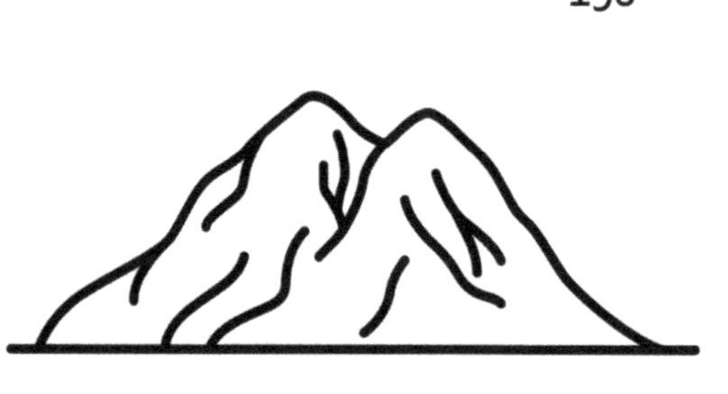

158

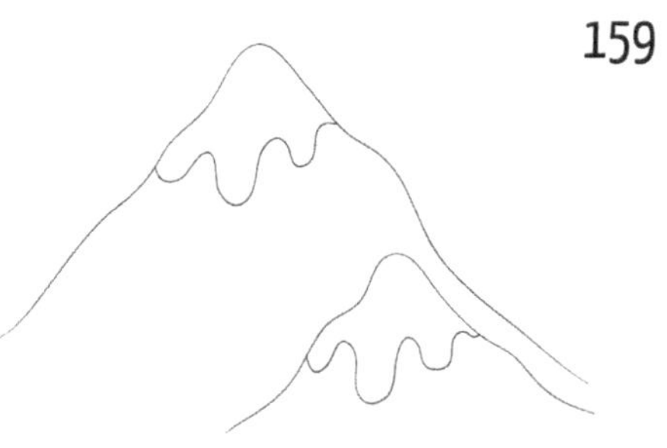

159

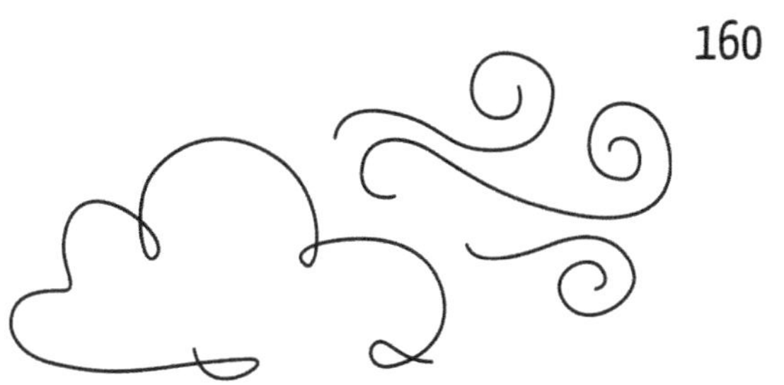

160

161

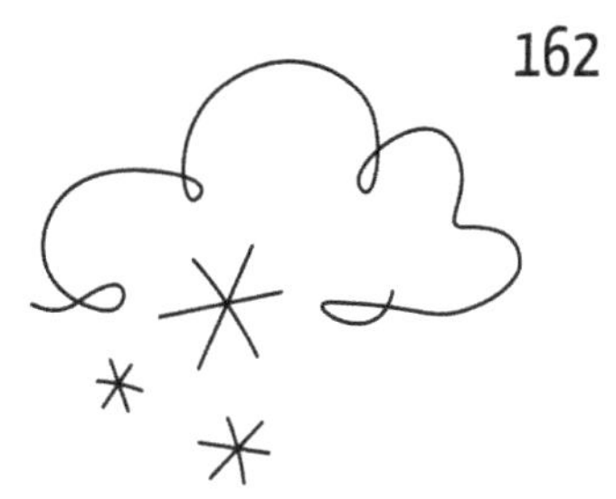

162

163

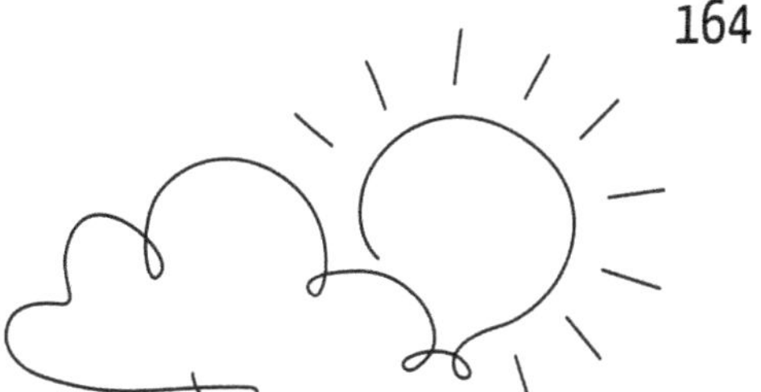

164

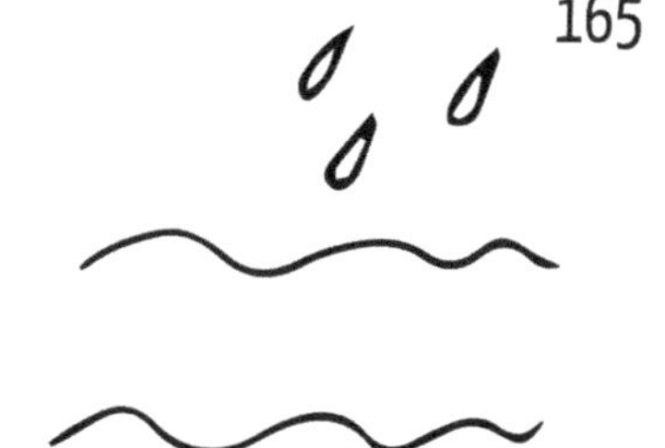

165

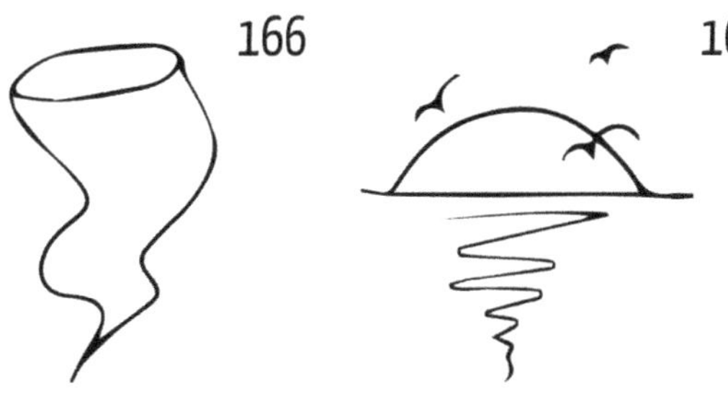

166

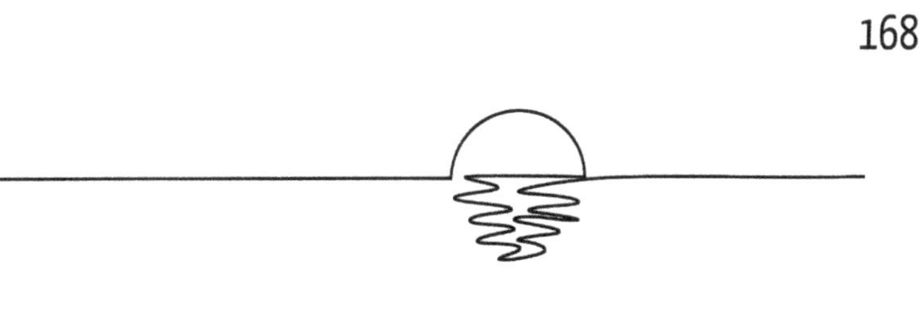

167 168

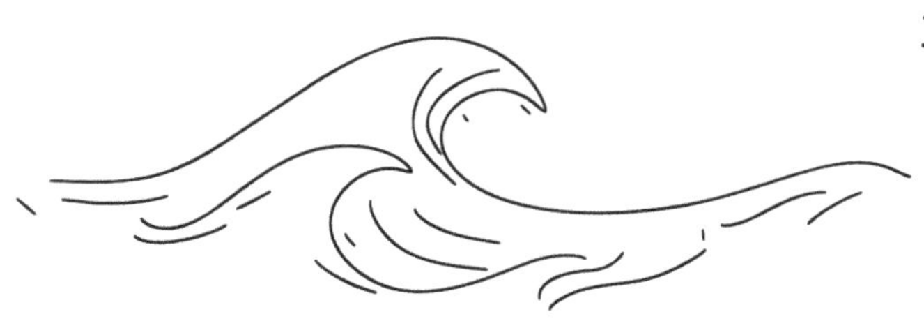

169

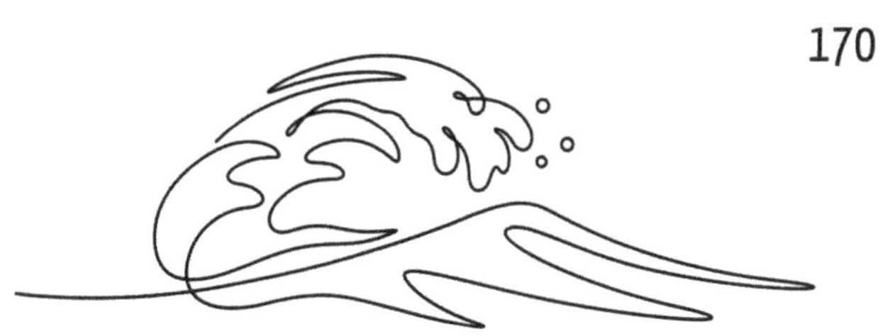

170

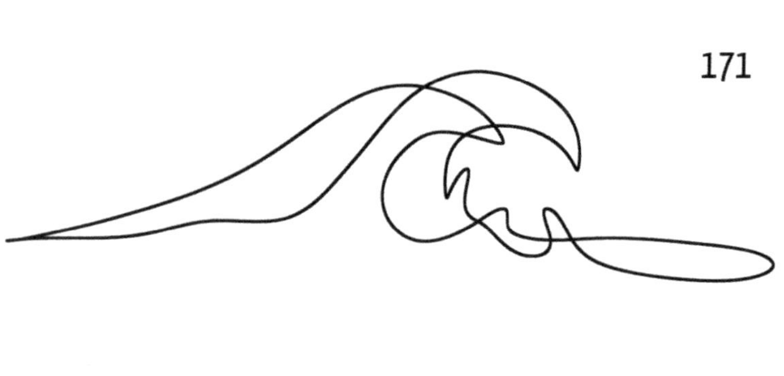

171

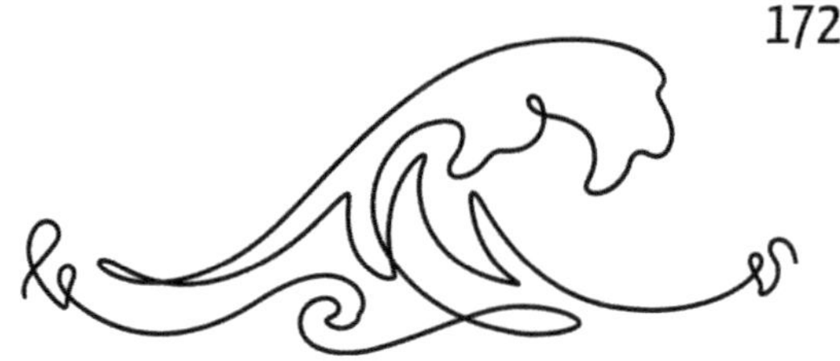

172

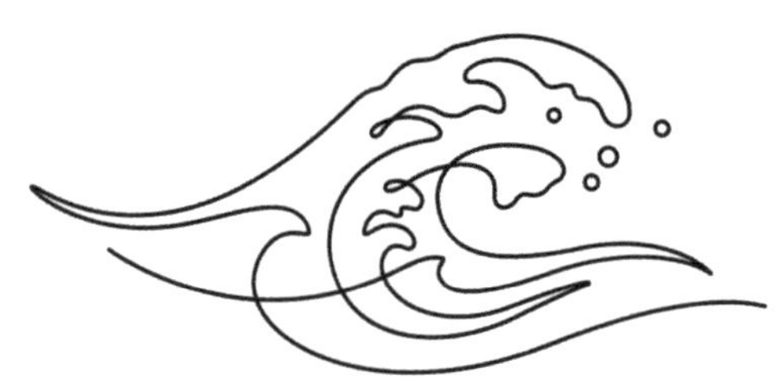

173

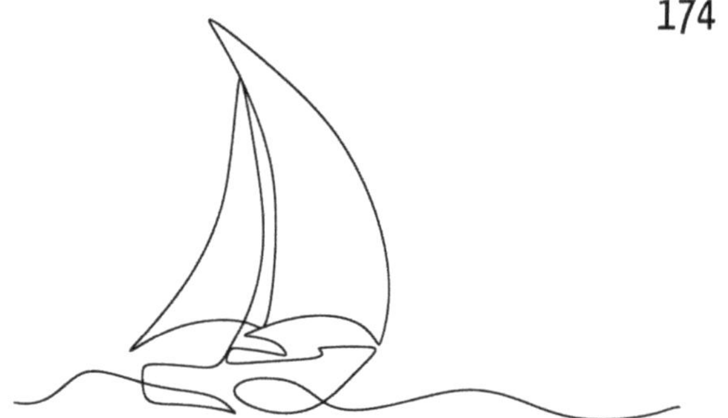

174

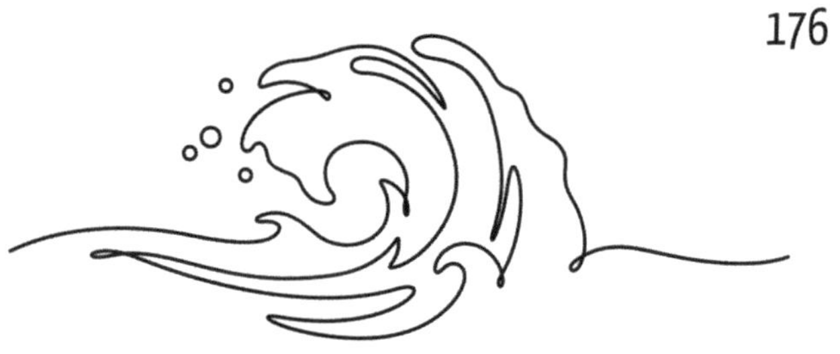

175

176

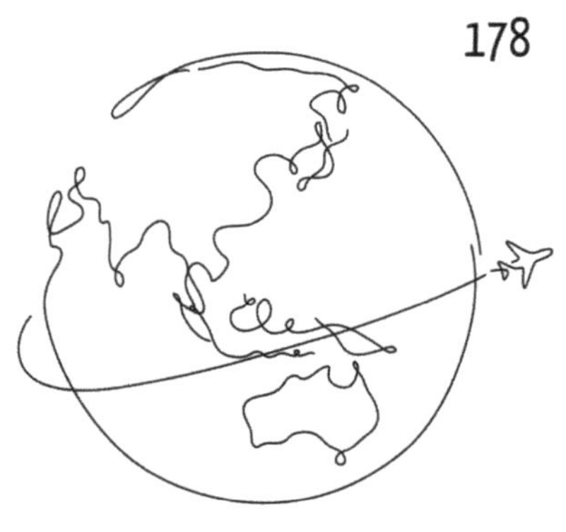

177

178

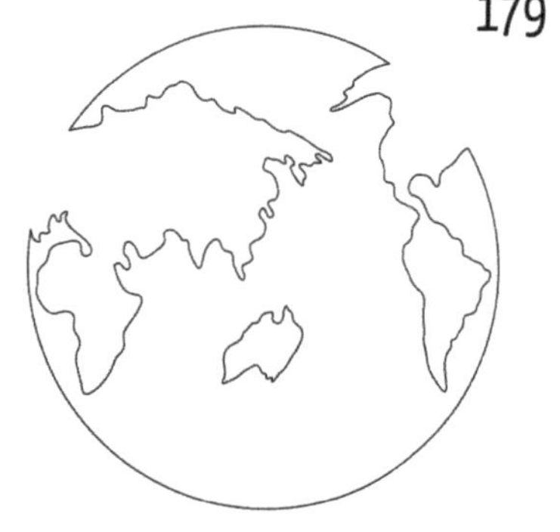

179

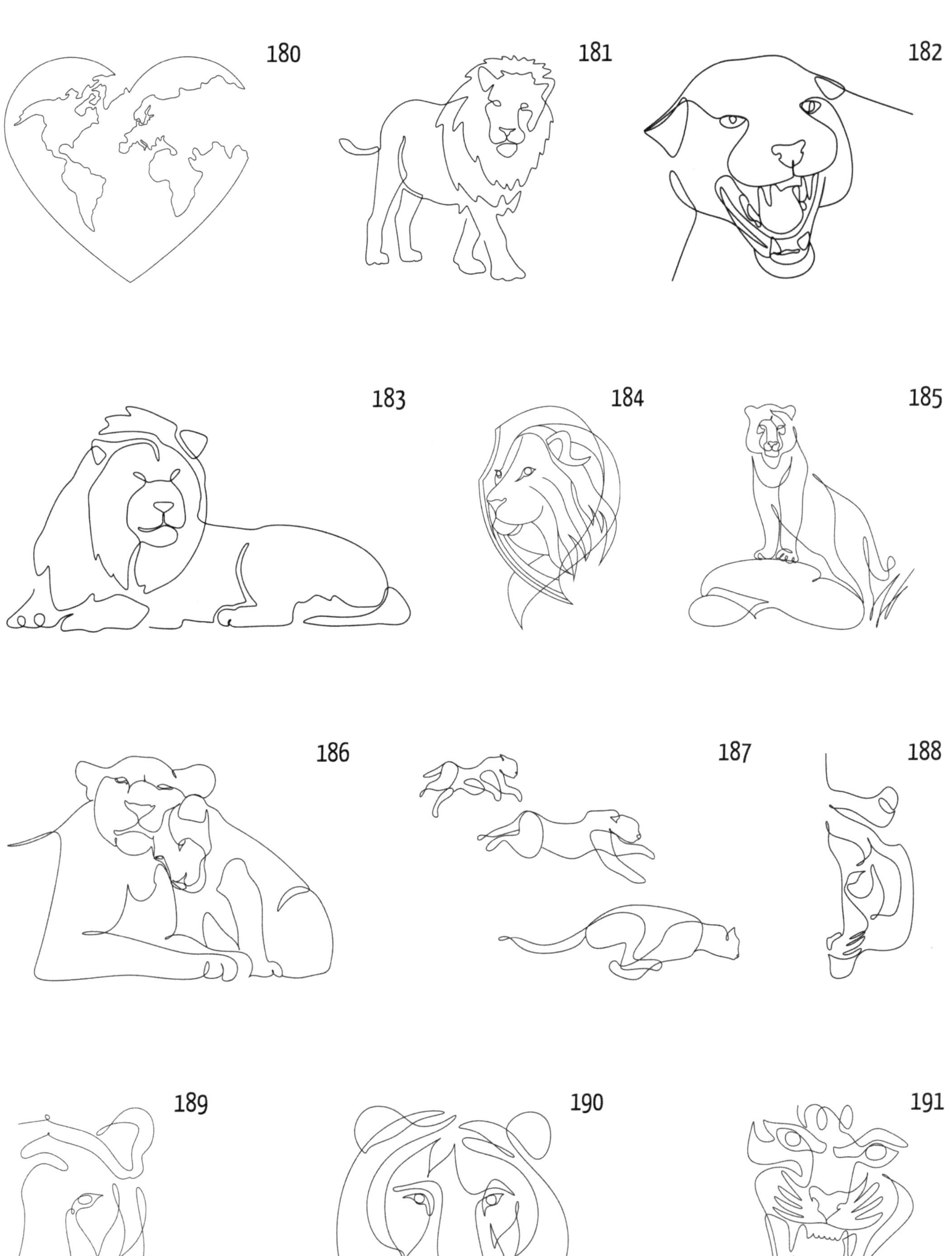

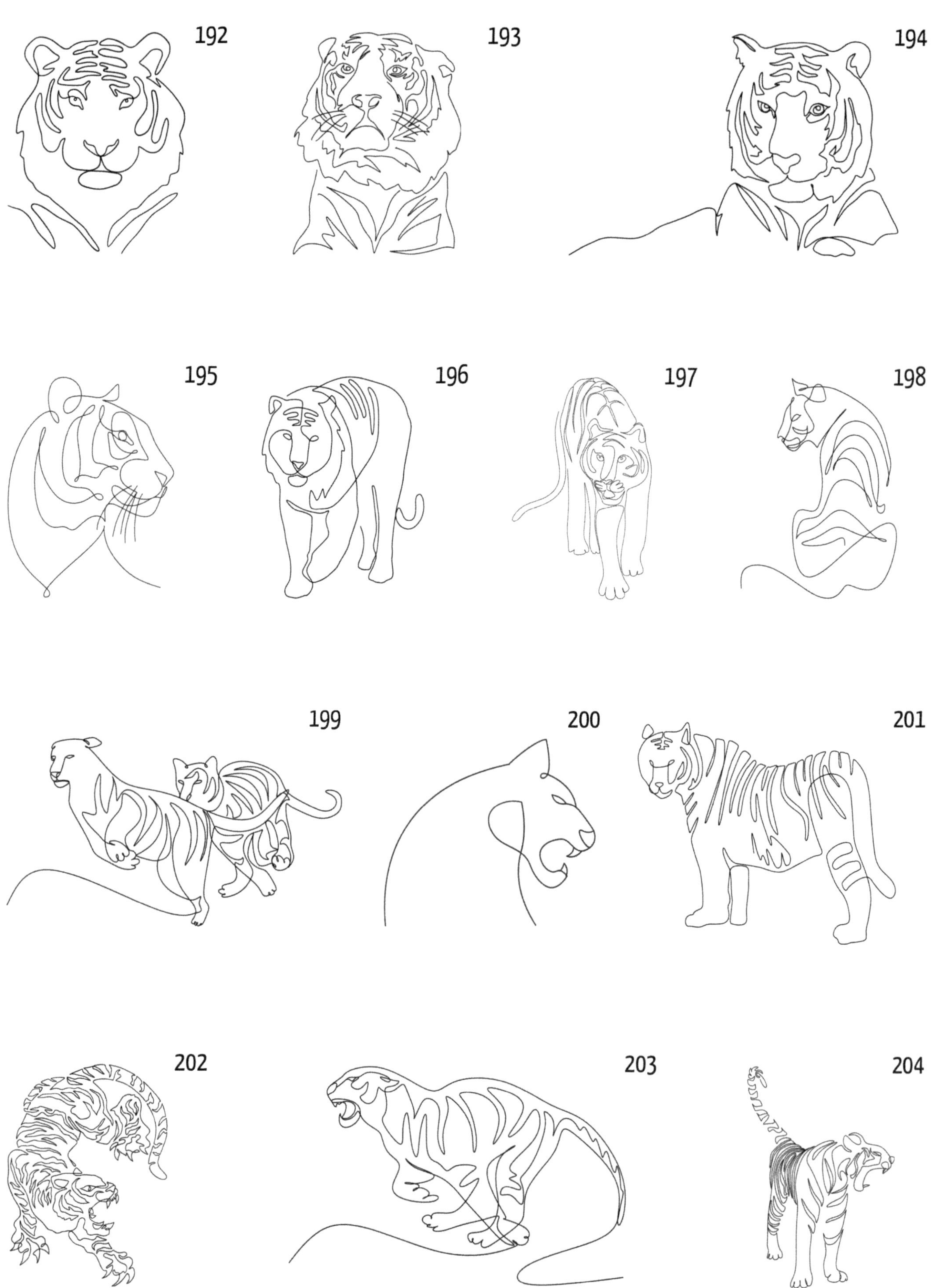

192
193
194
195
196
197
198
199
200
201
202
203
204

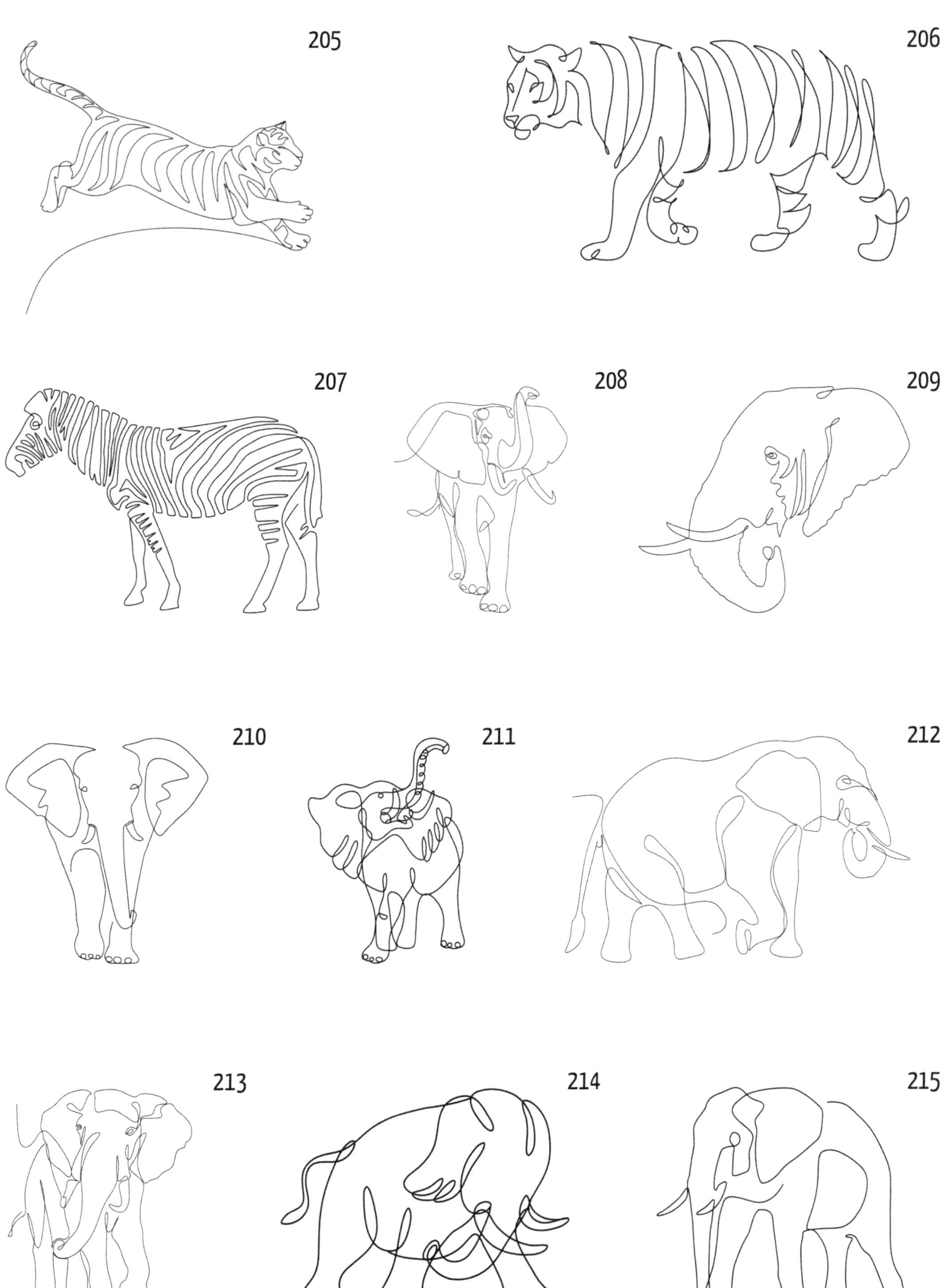

205
206
207
208
209
210
211
212
213
214
215

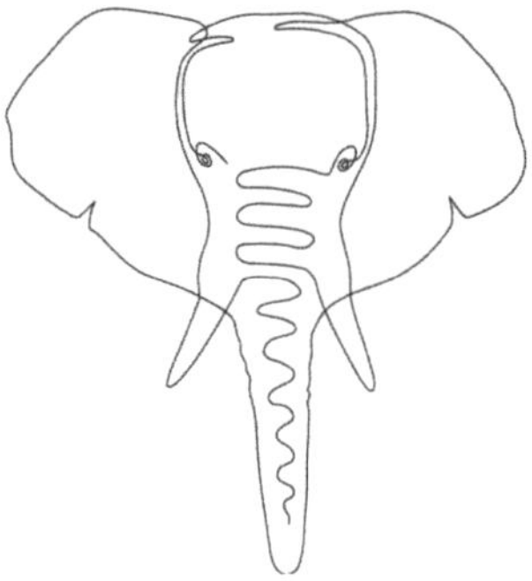

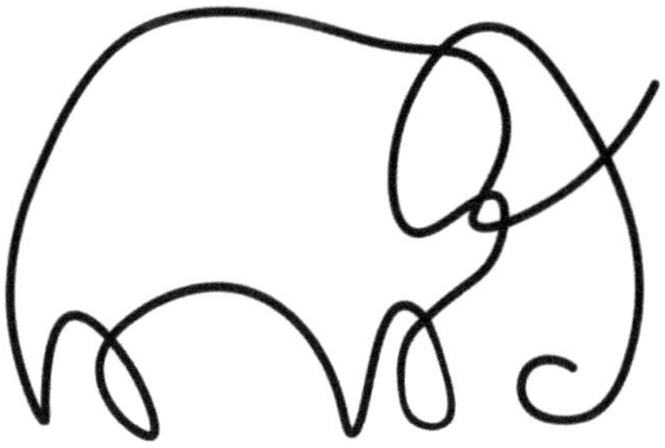

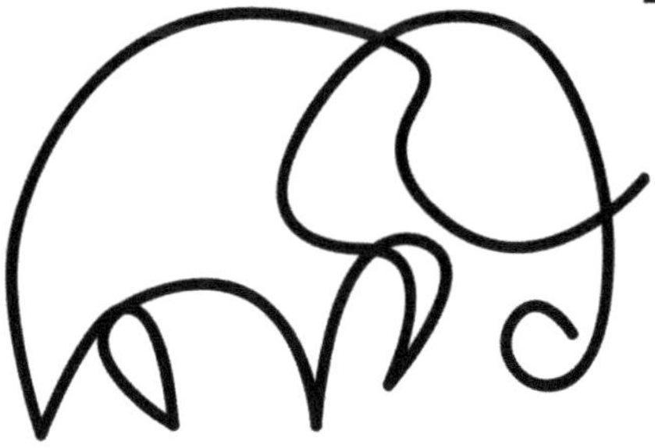

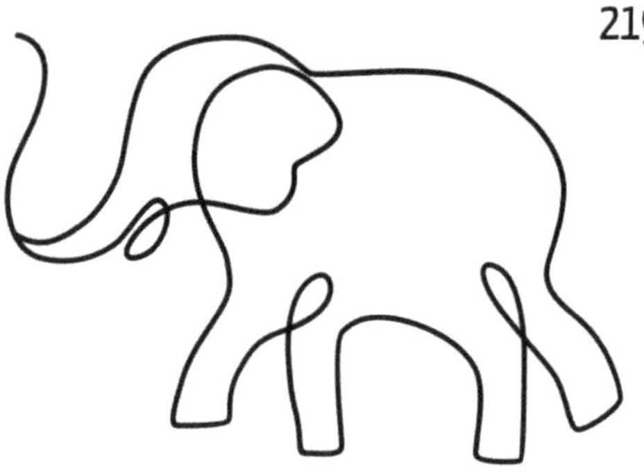

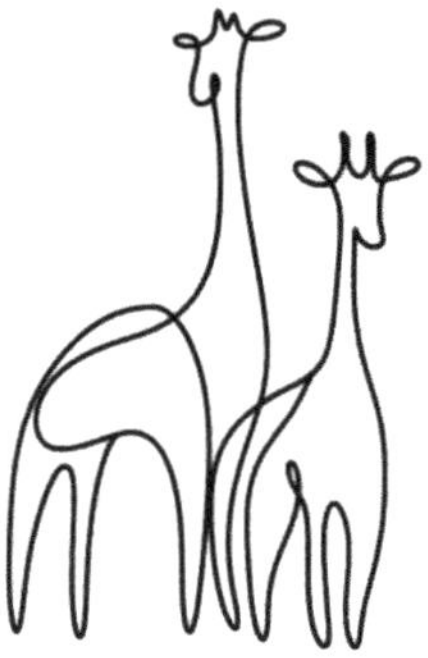

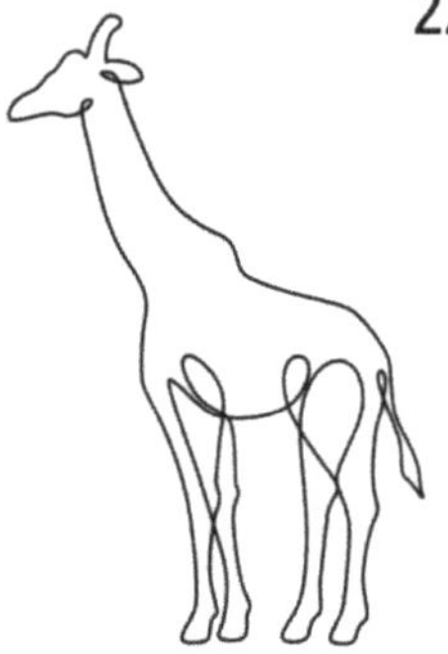

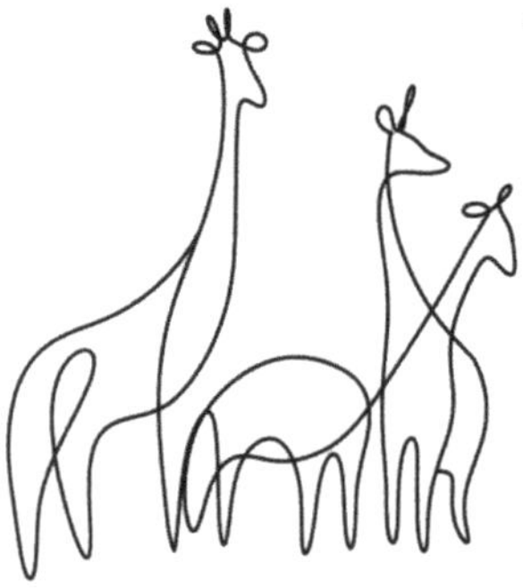

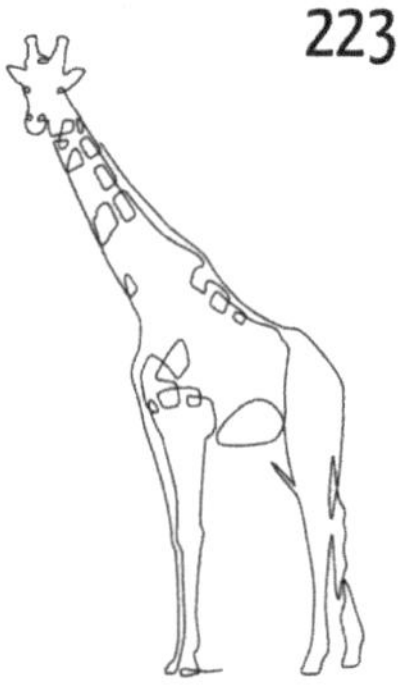

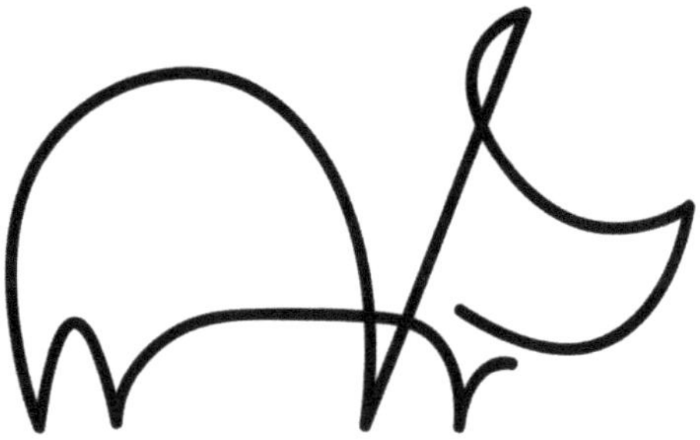

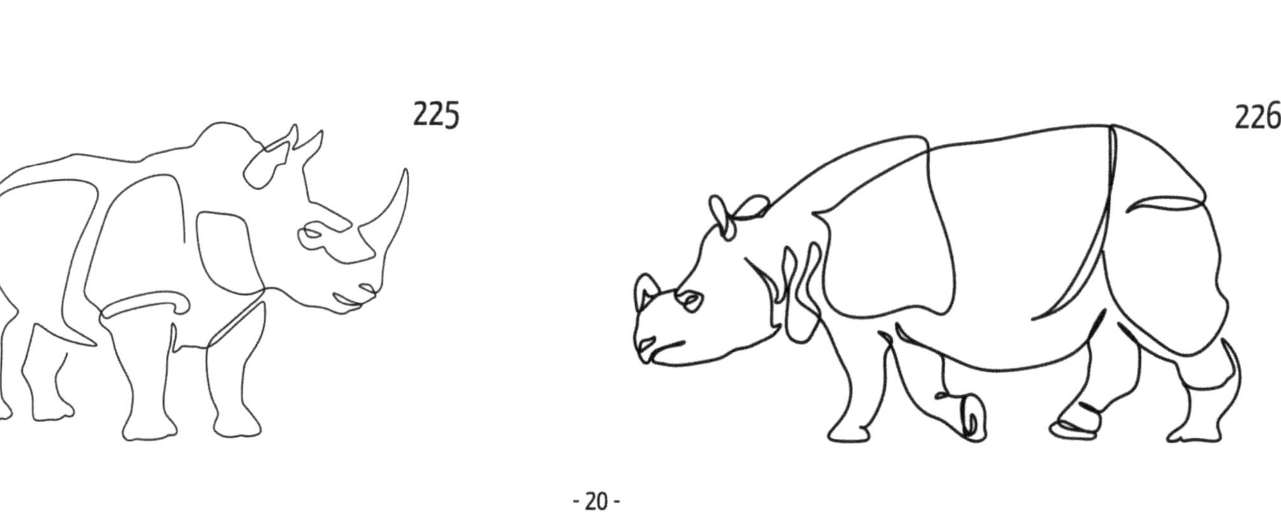

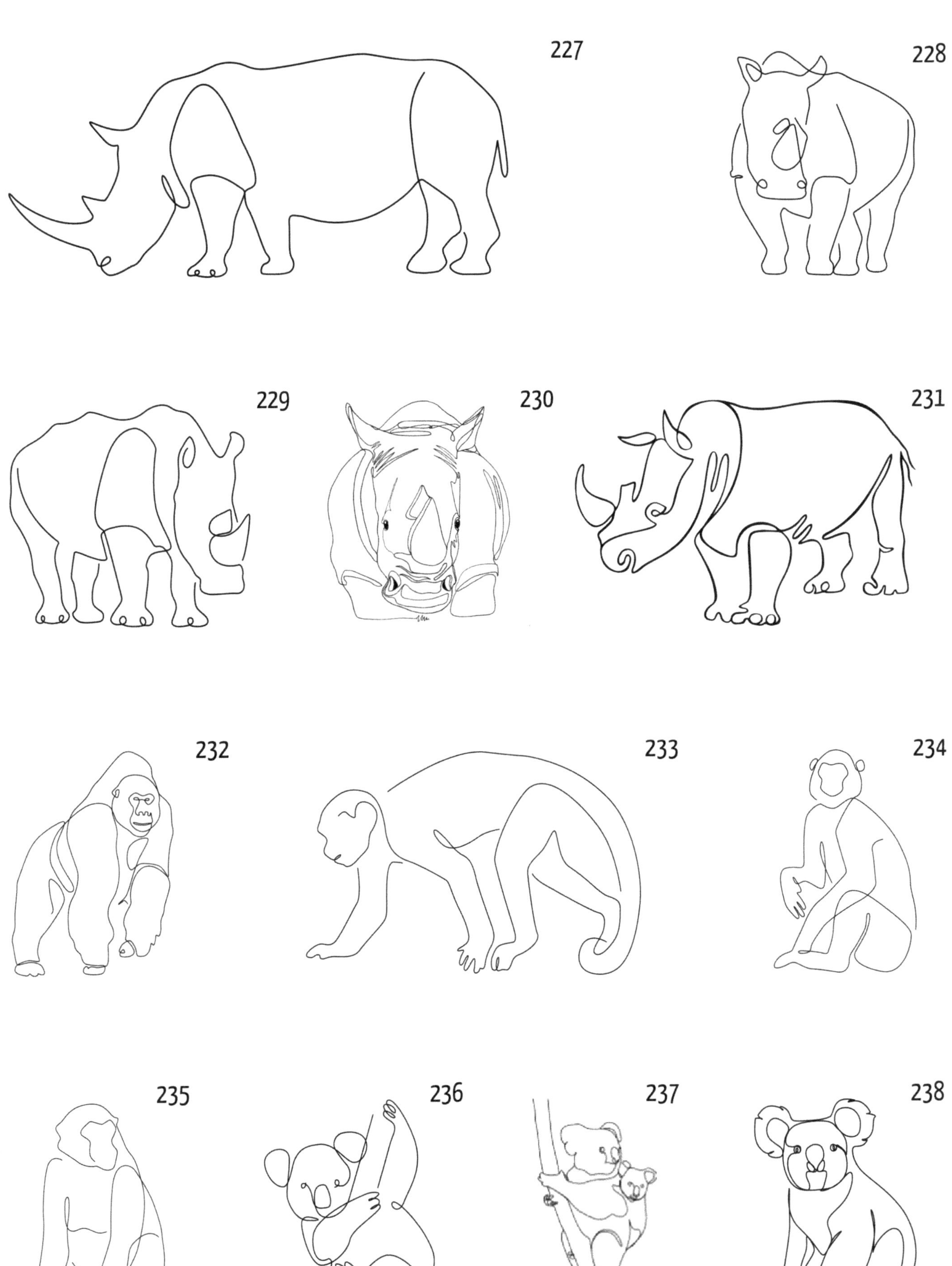

227

228

229

230

231

232

233

234

235

236

237

238

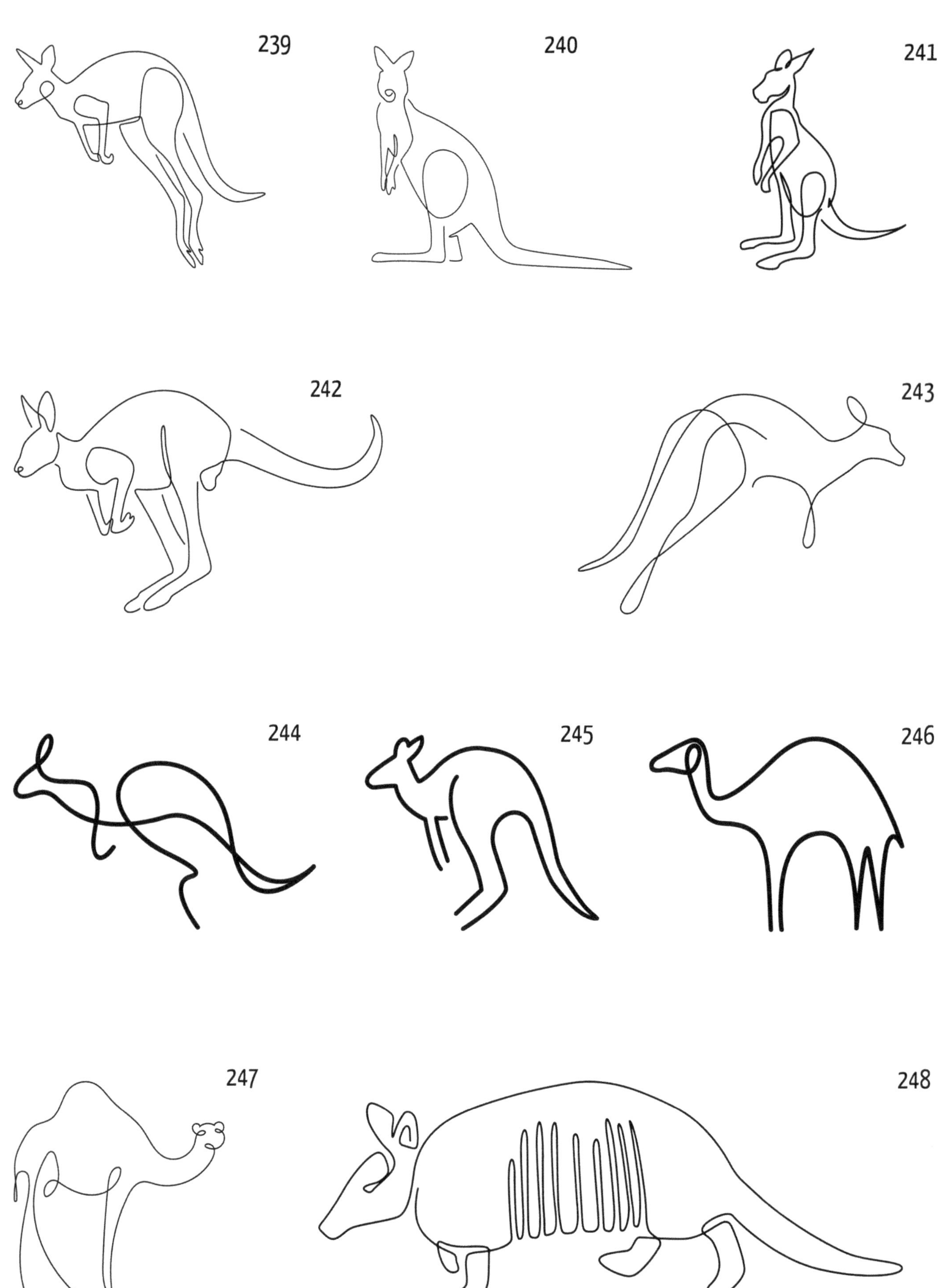

239
240
241
242
243
244
245
246
247
248

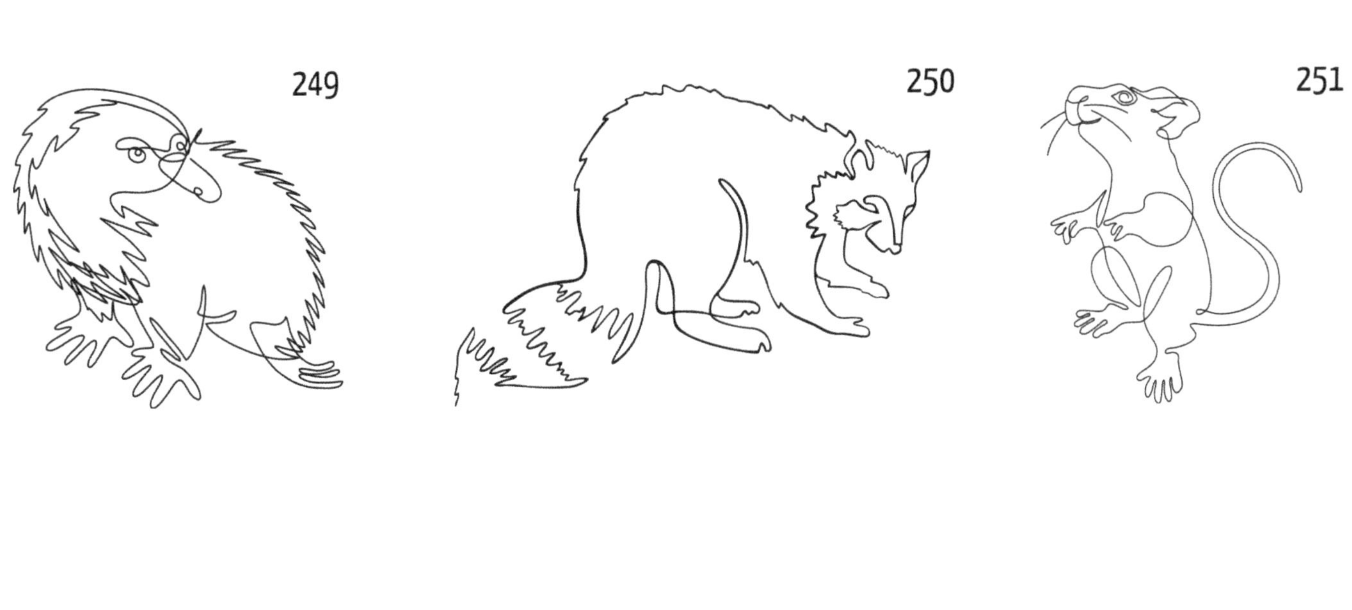

249
250
251

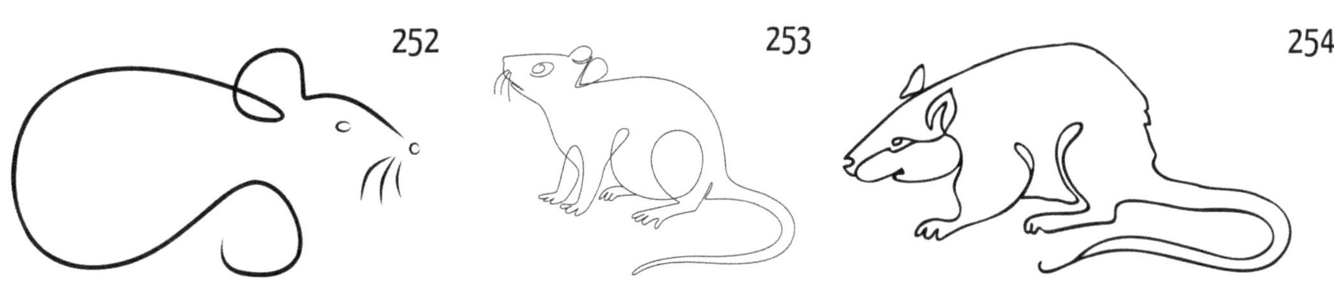

252
253
254

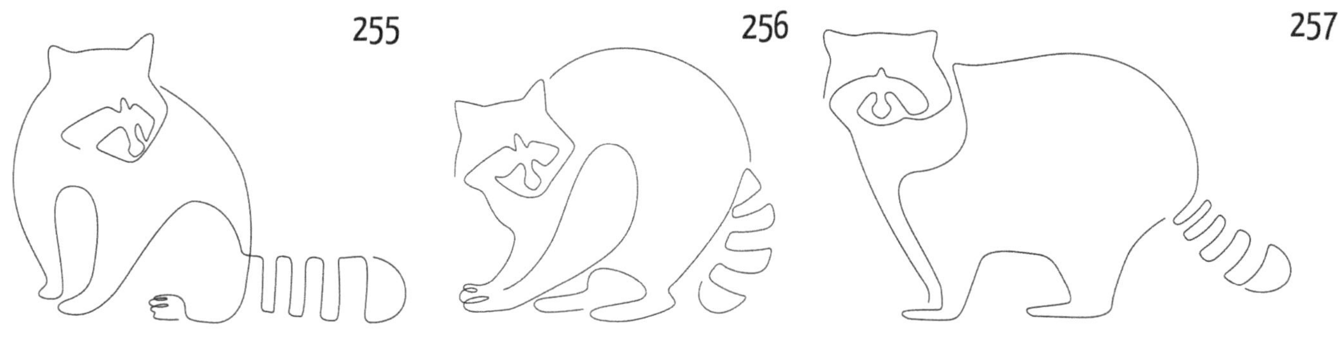

255
256
257

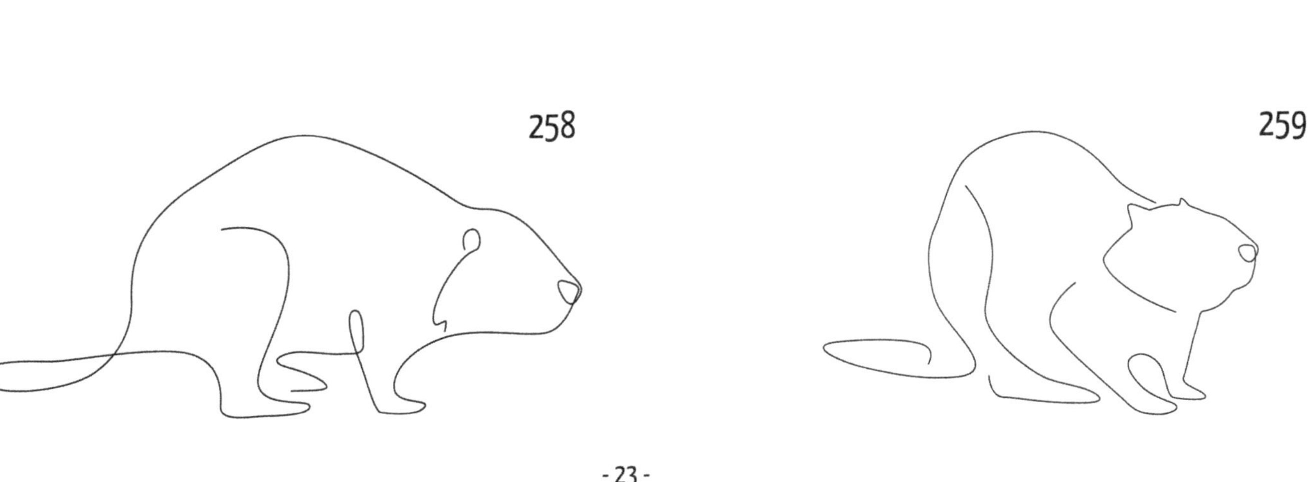

258
259

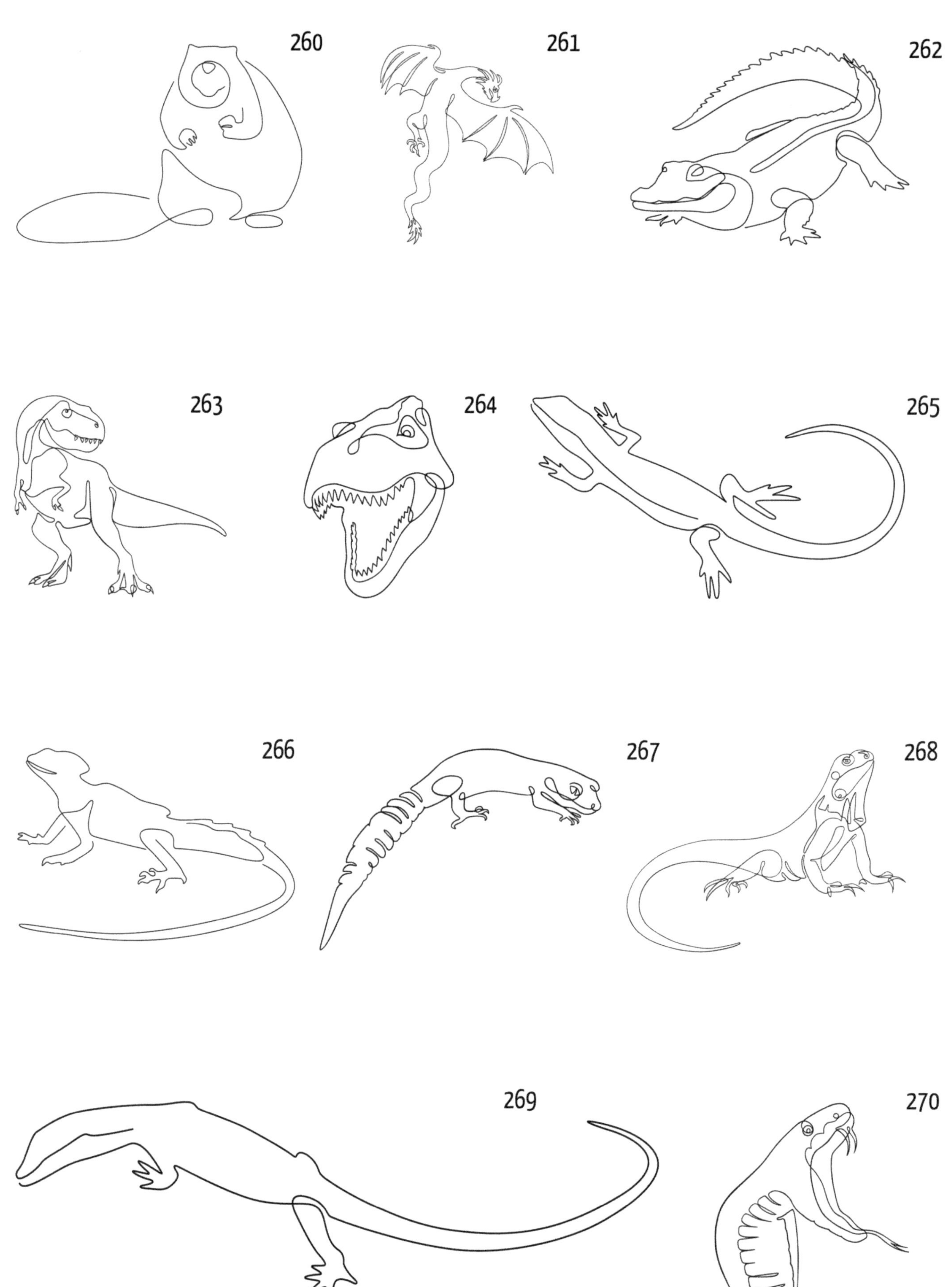

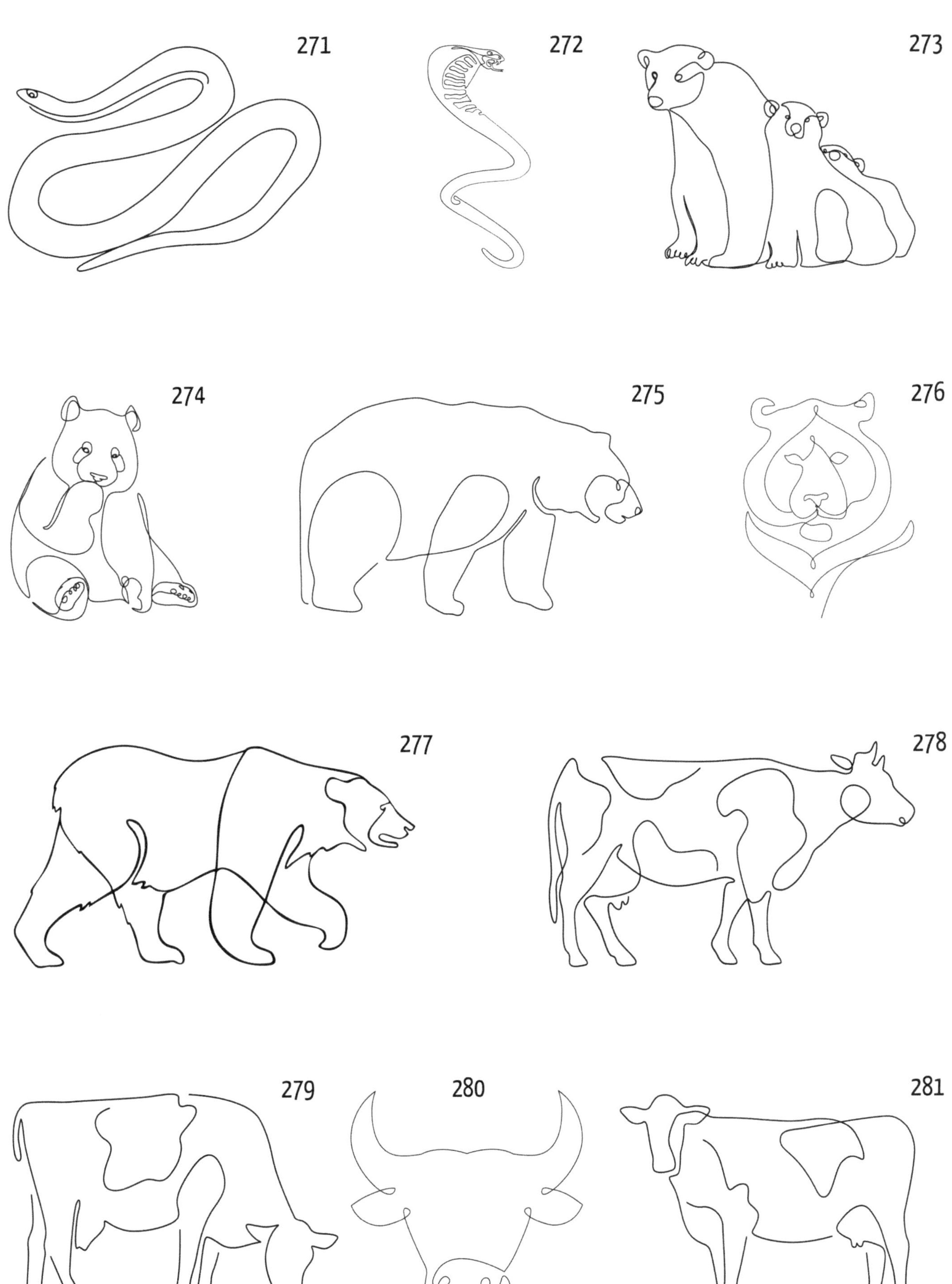

271
272
273
274
275
276
277
278
279
280
281

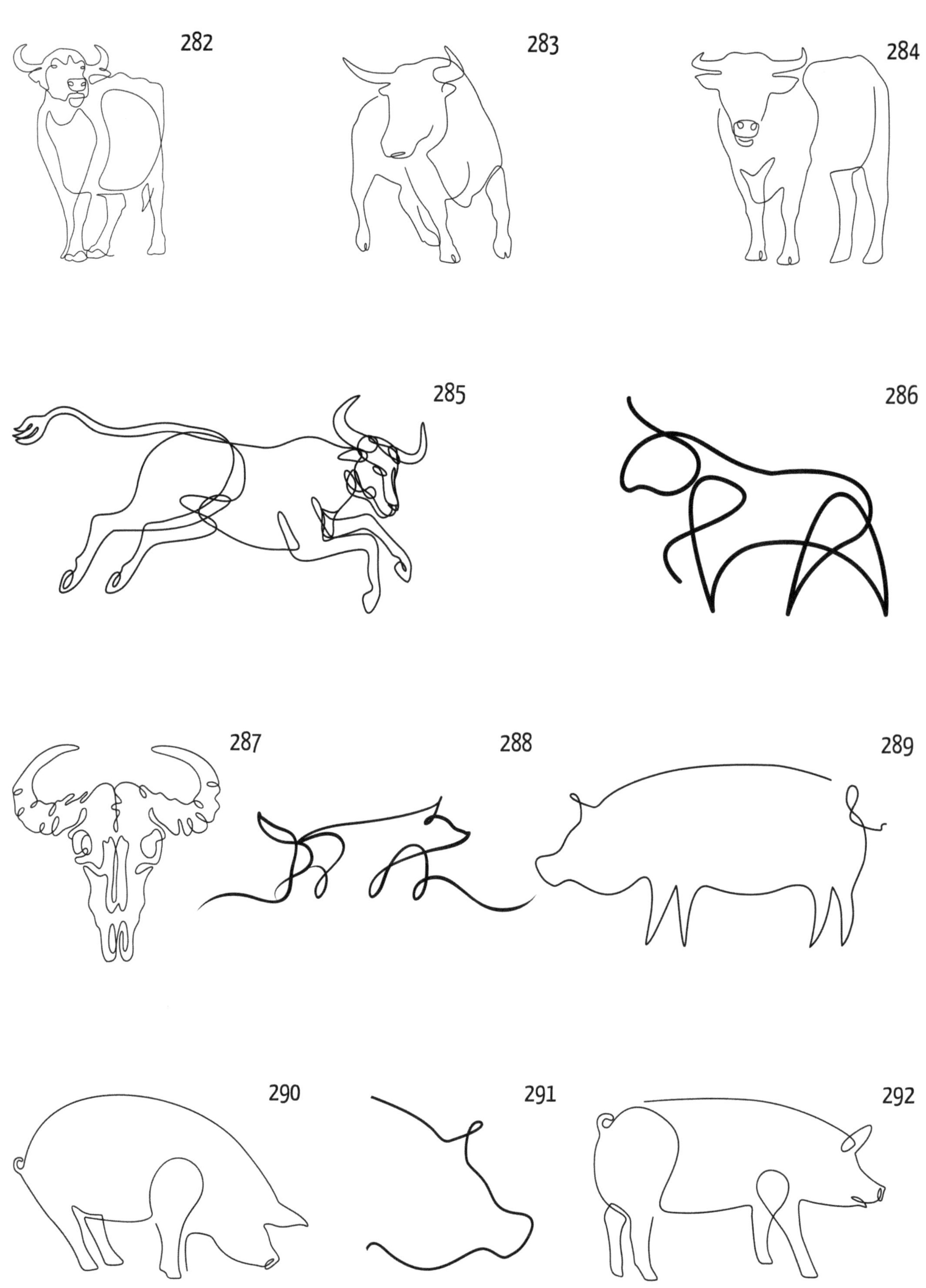

282
283
284
285
286
287
288
289
290
291
292

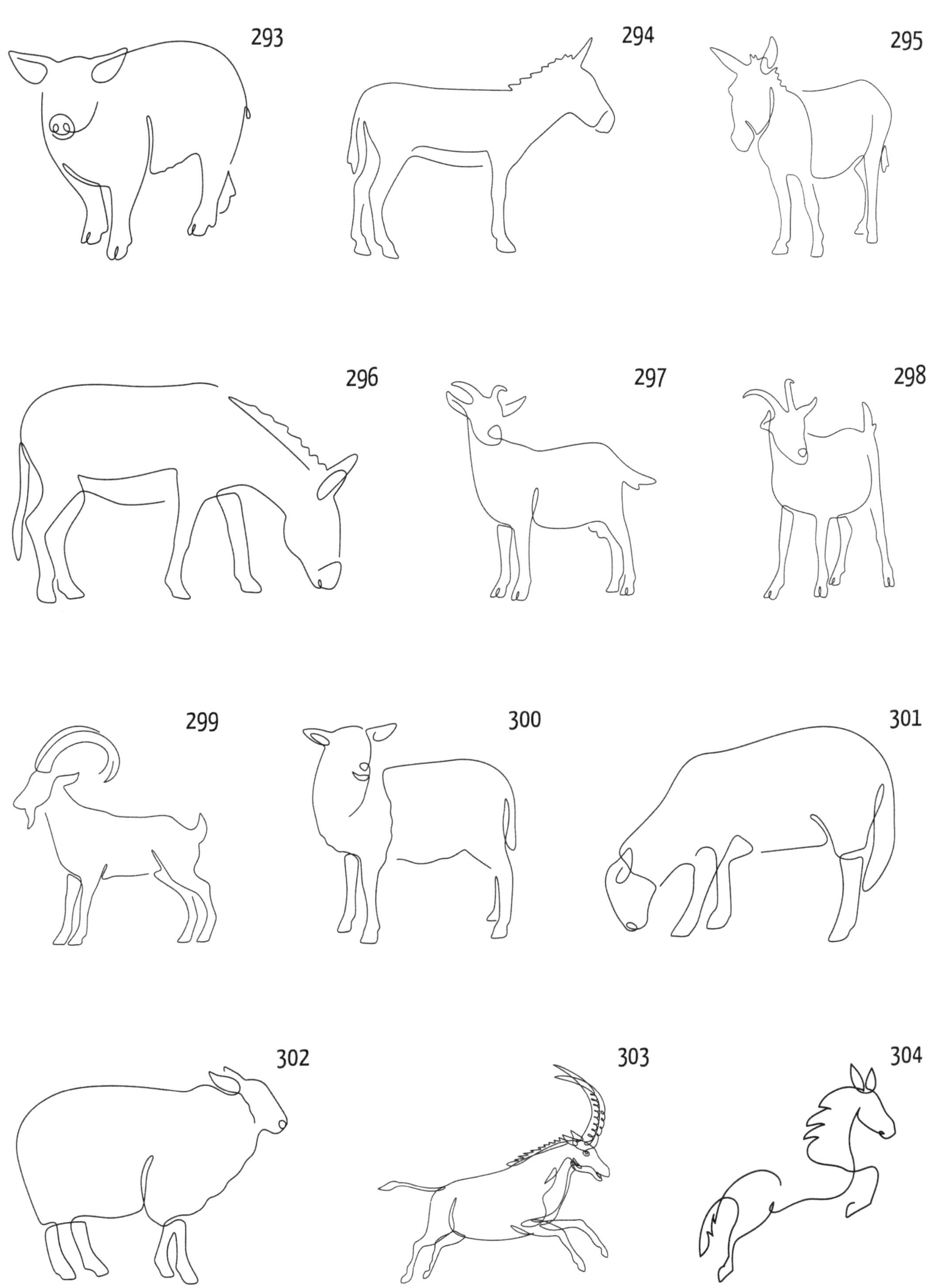

293
294
295
296
297
298
299
300
301
302
303
304

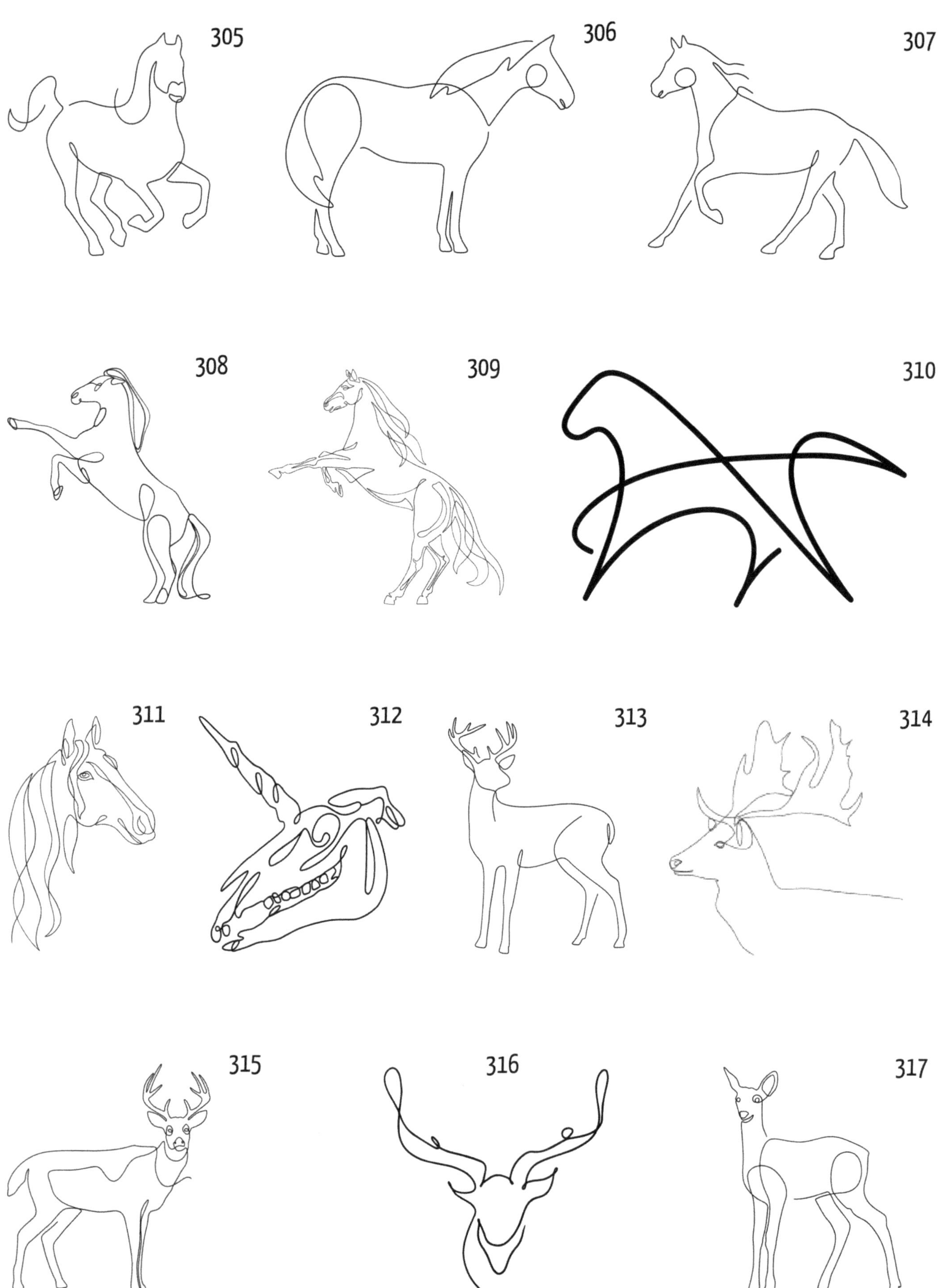
305
306
307
308
309
310
311
312
313
314
315
316
317

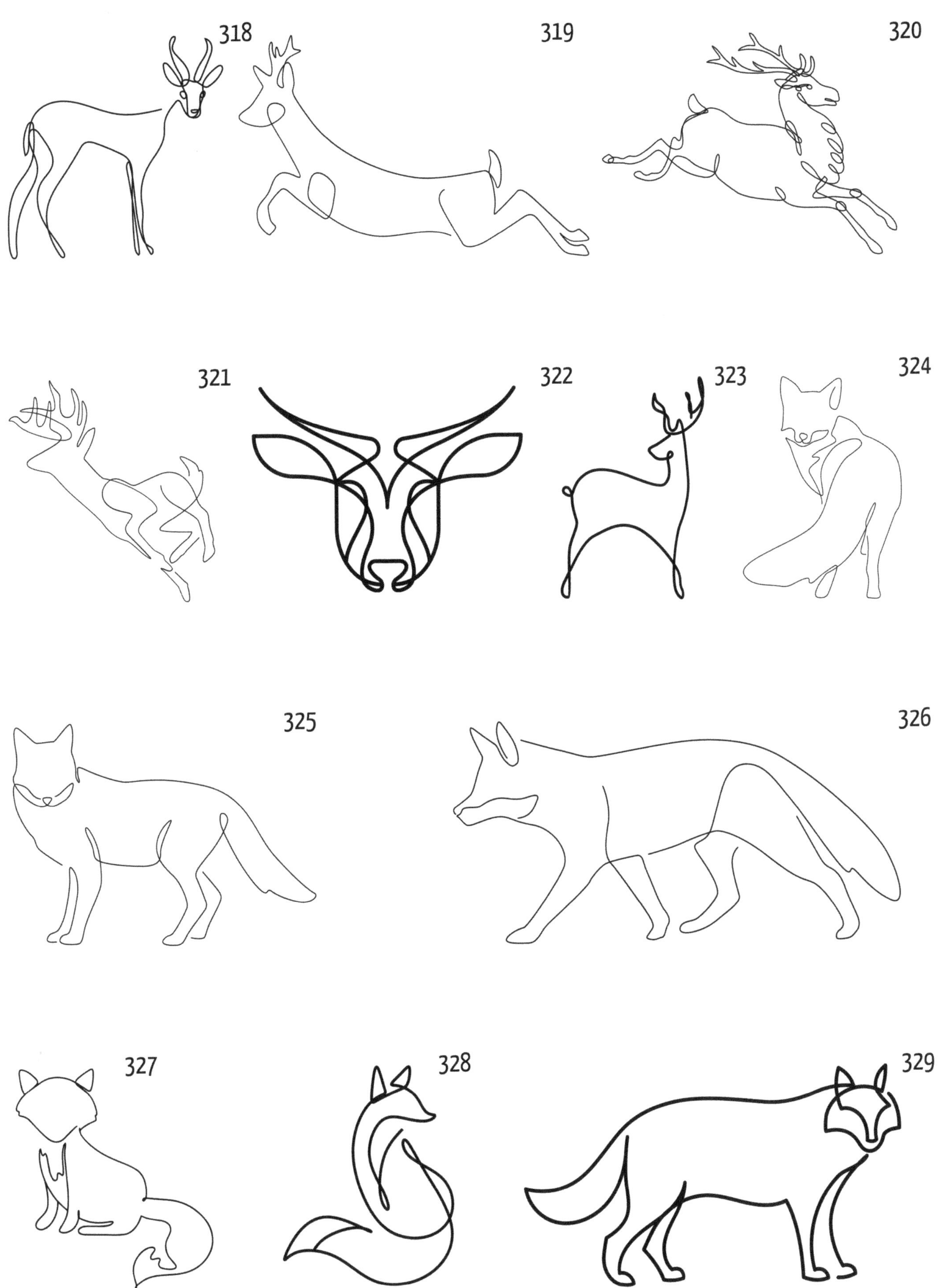

318
319
320
321
322
323
324
325
326
327
328
329

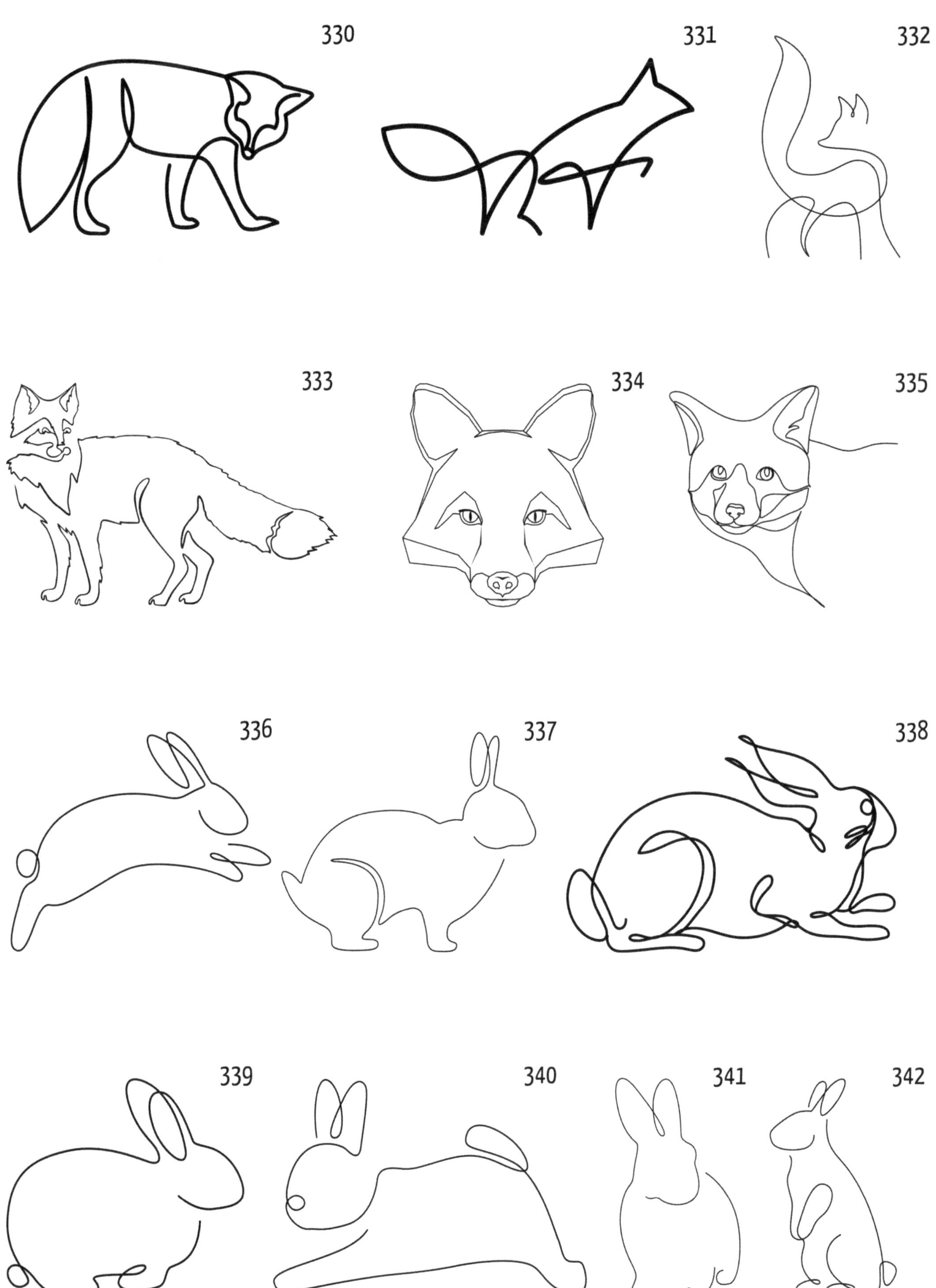

330
331
332
333
334
335
336
337
338
339
340
341
342

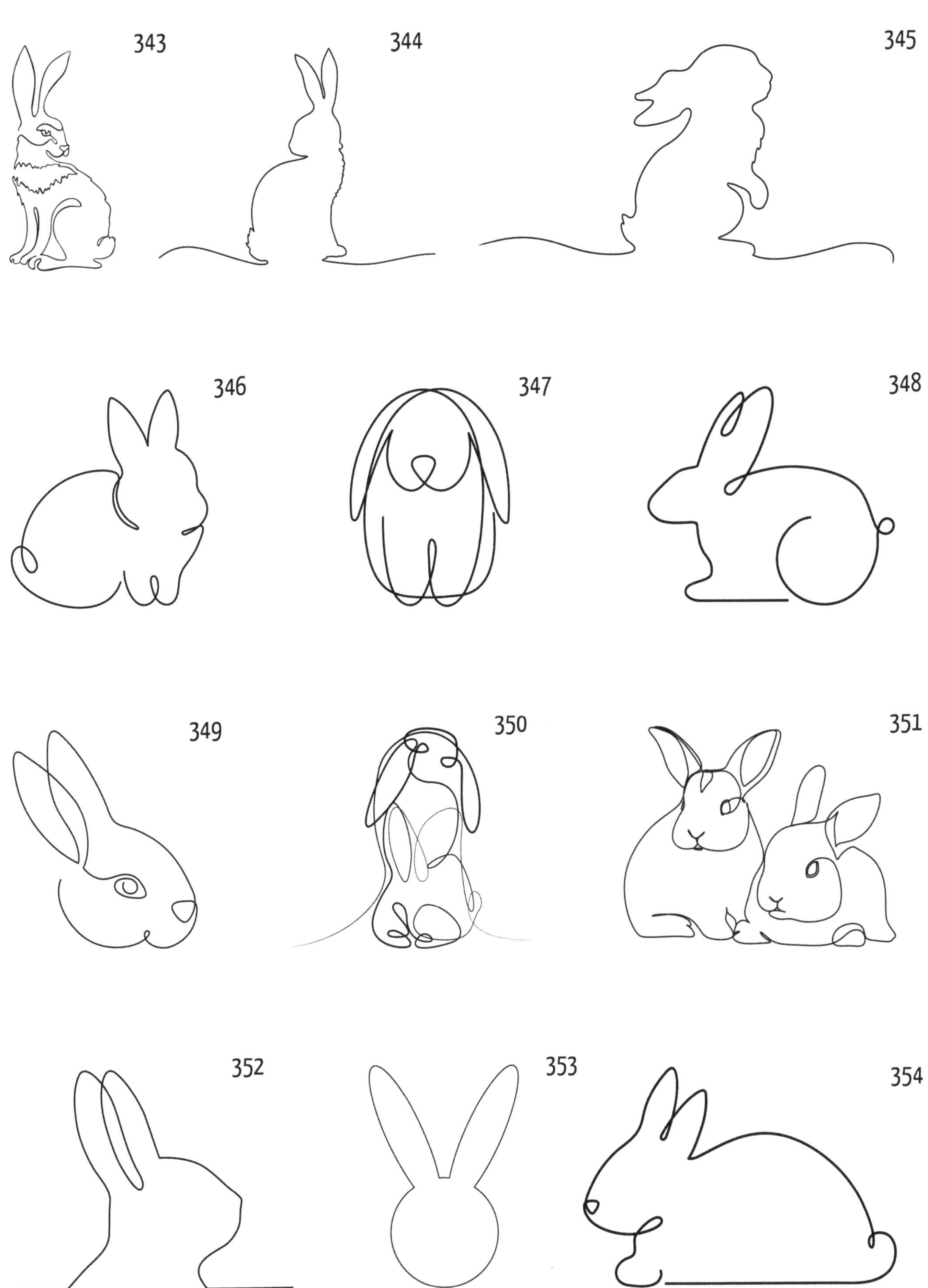

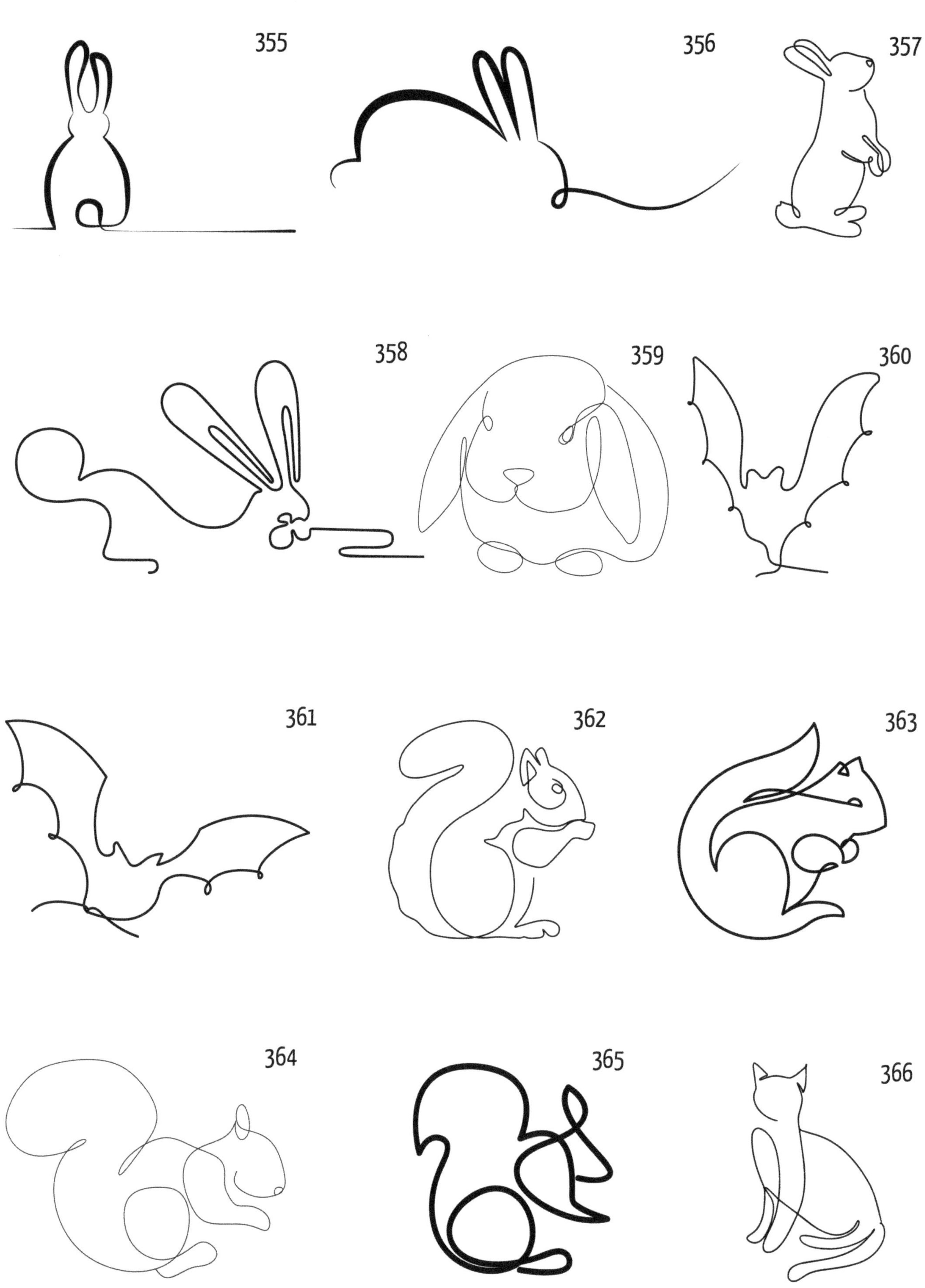

355
356
357
358
359
360
361
362
363
364
365
366

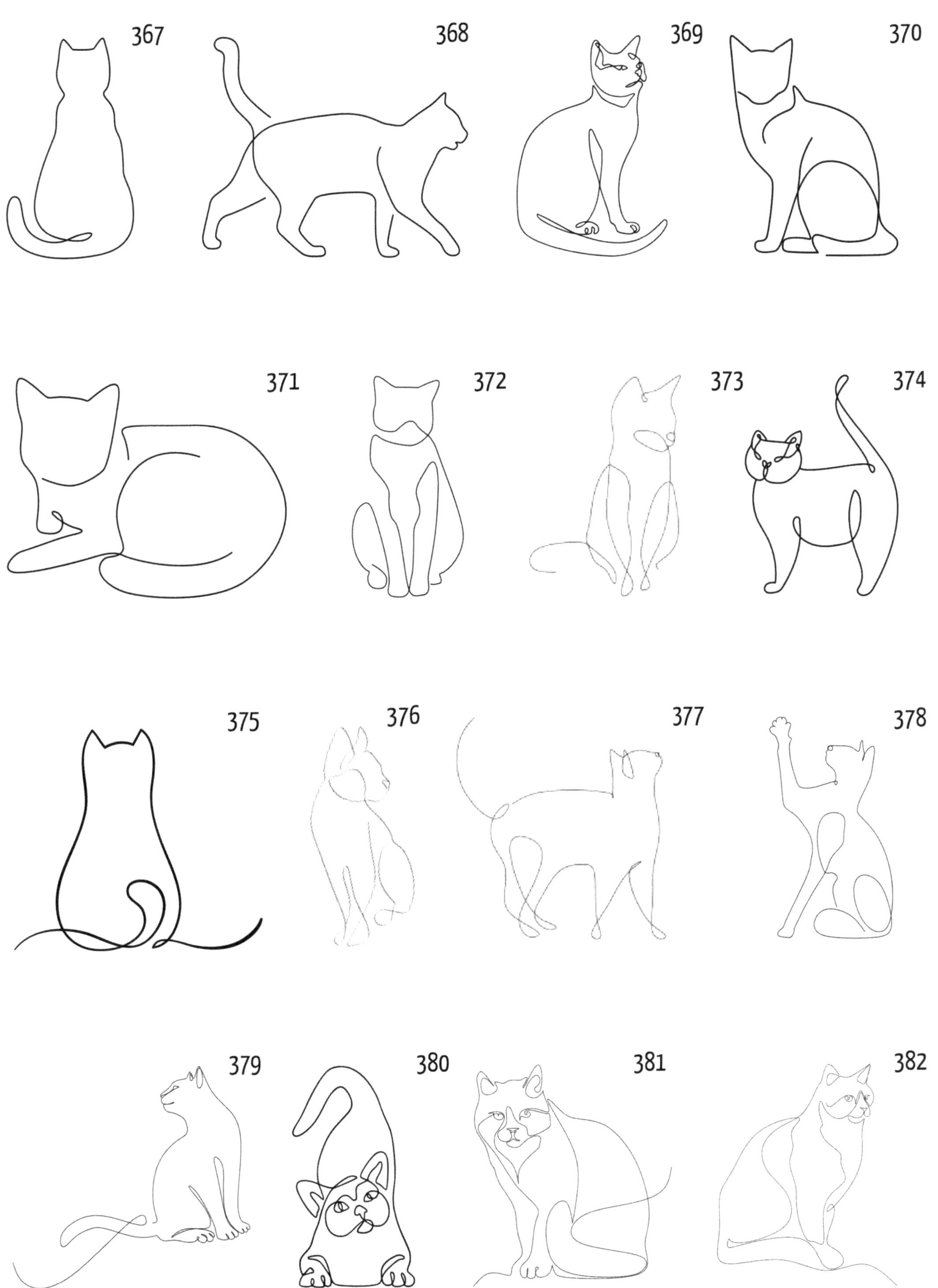

367
368
369
370
371
372
373
374
375
376
377
378
379
380
381
382

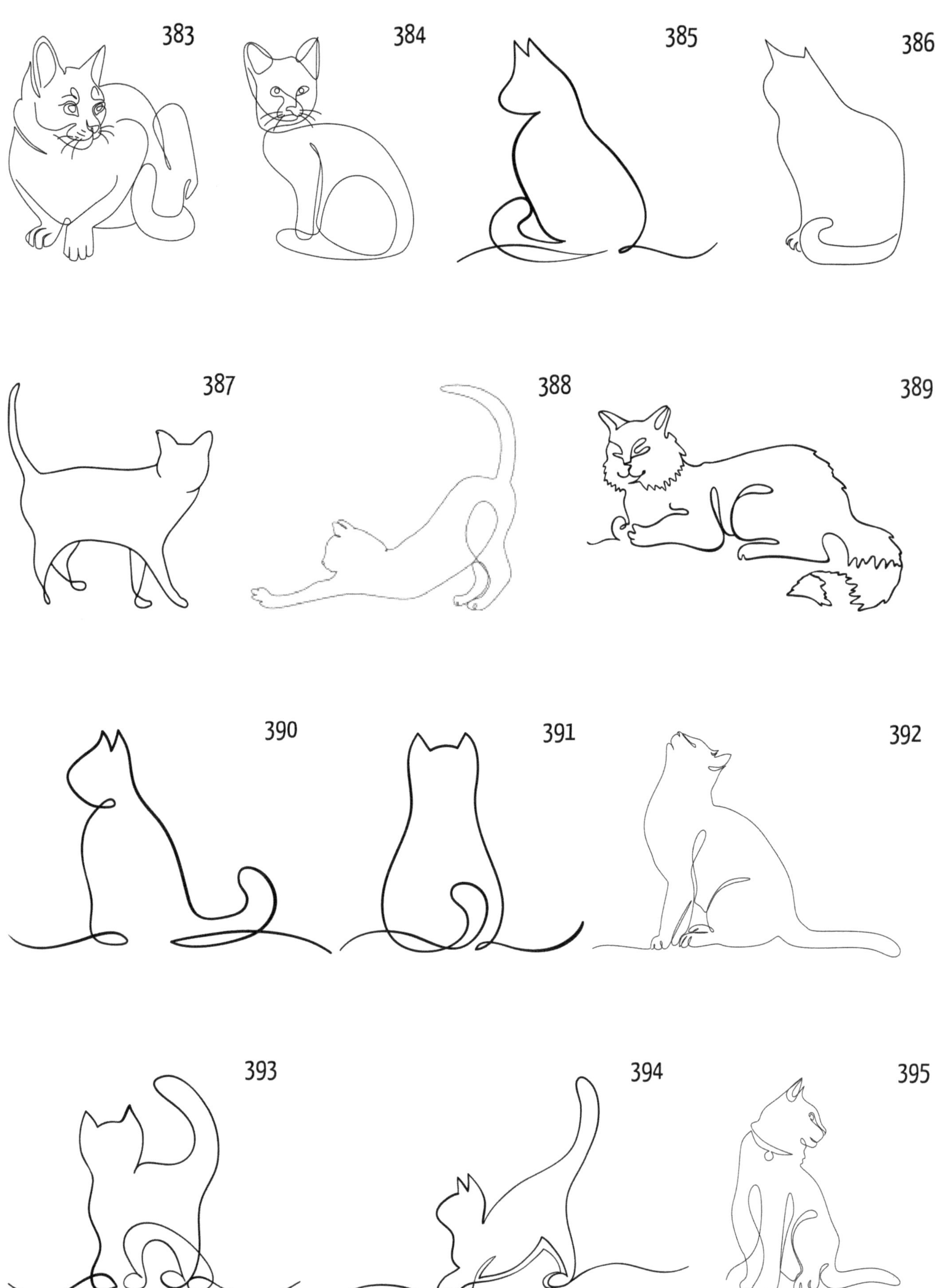
383
384
385
386
387
388
389
390
391
392
393
394
395

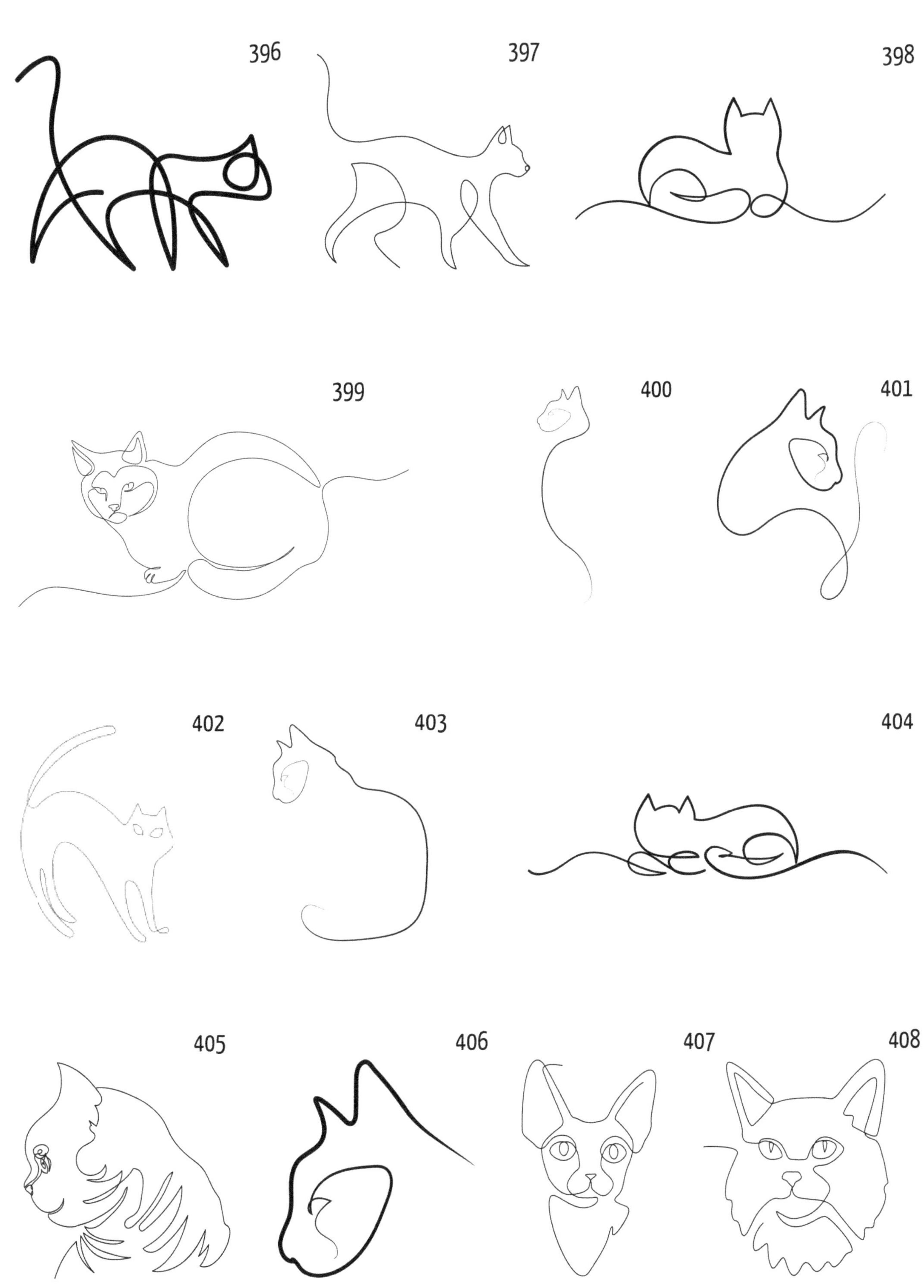

396
397
398
399
400
401
402
403
404
405
406
407
408

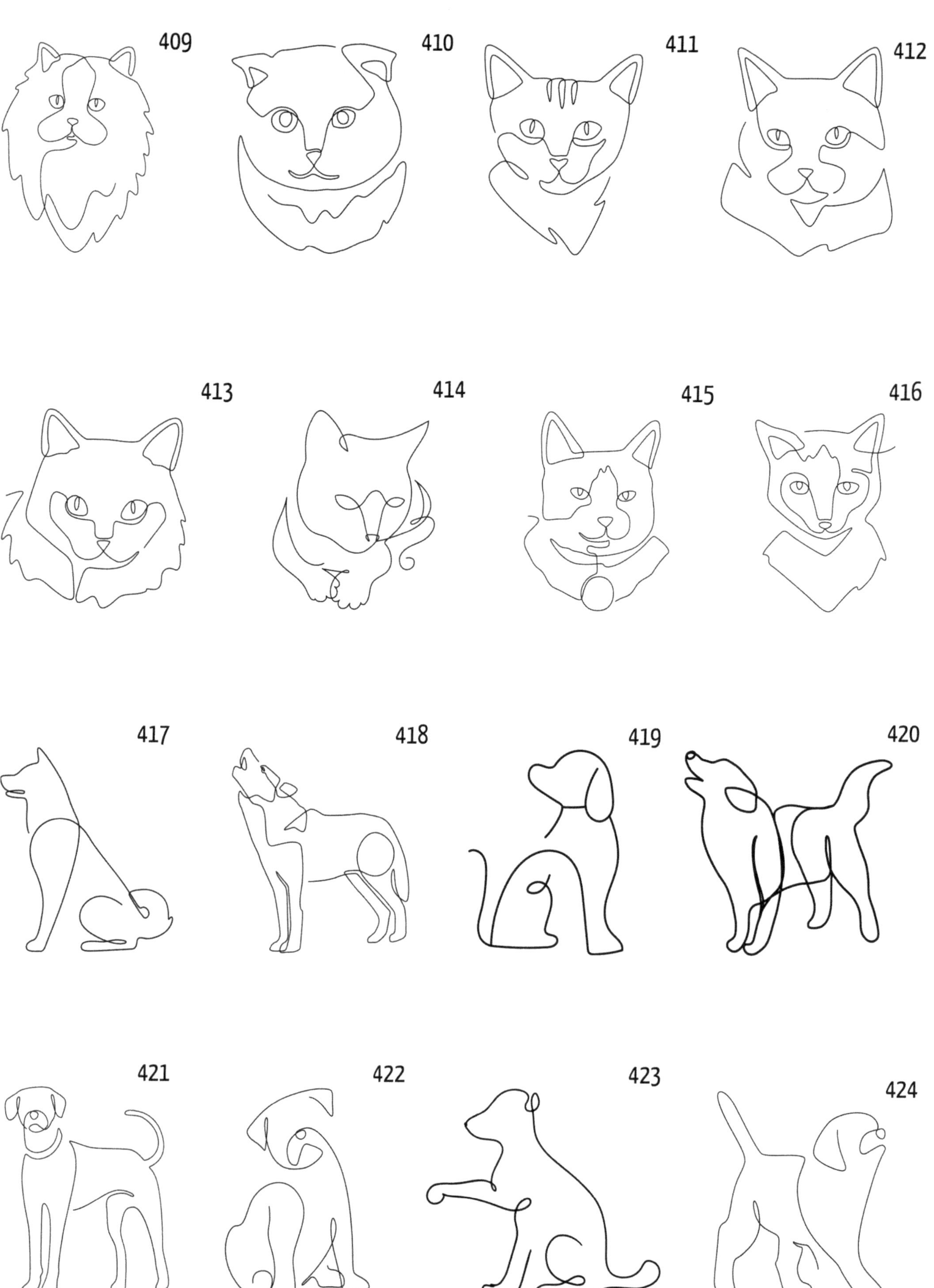

409
410
411
412
413
414
415
416
417
418
419
420
421
422
423
424

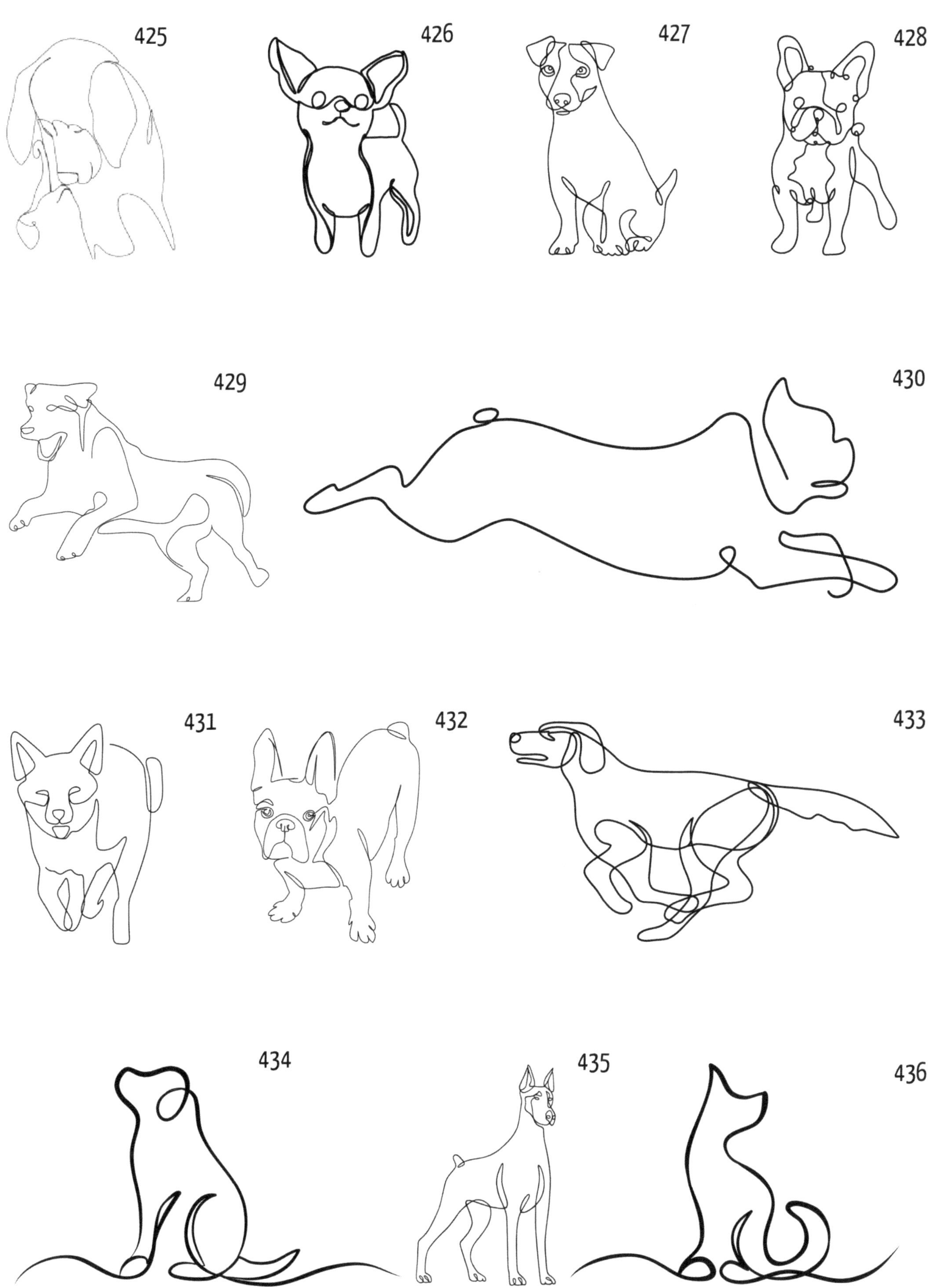

425   426   427   428

429   430

431   432   433

434   435   436

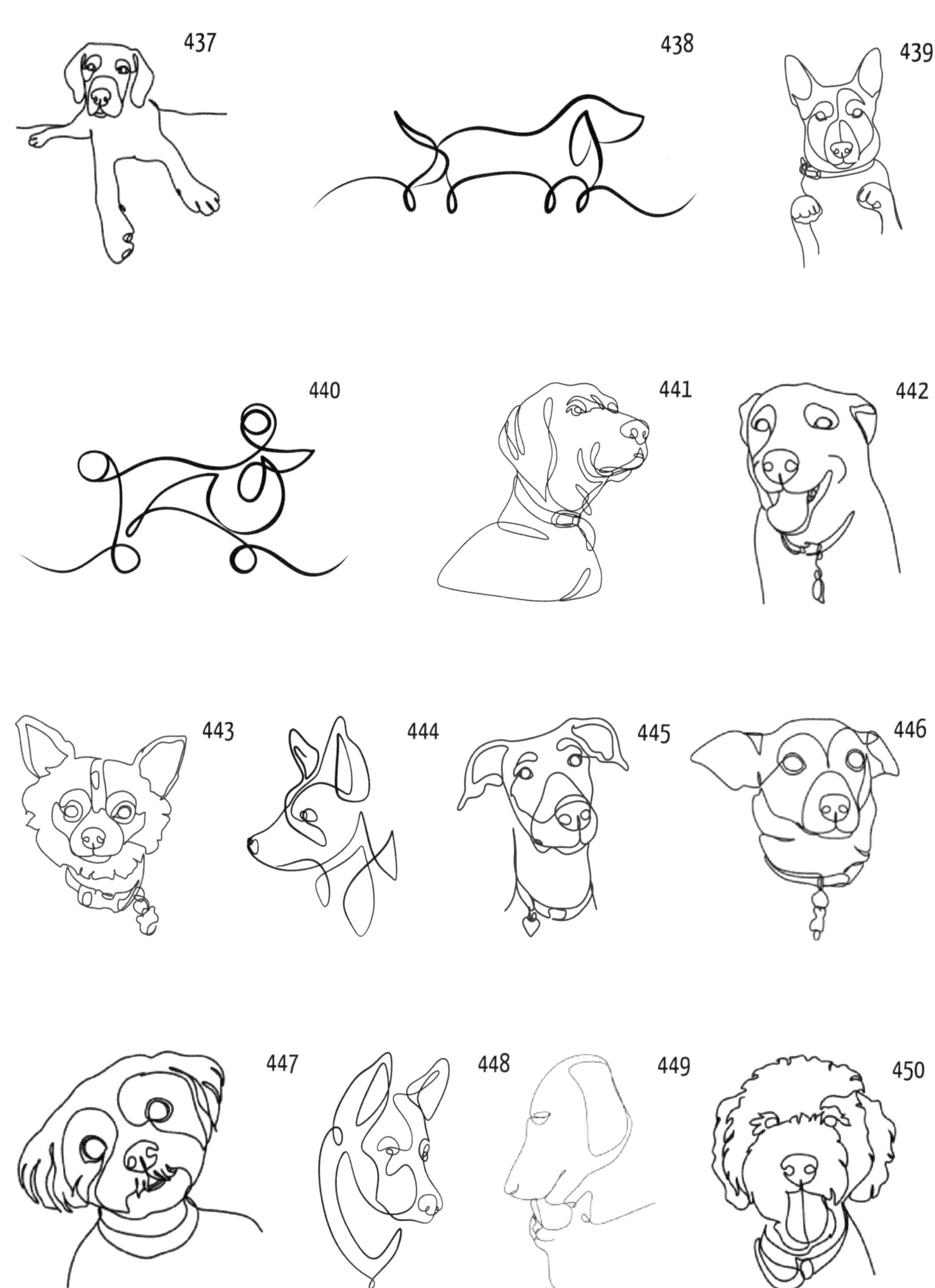

437
438
439
440
441
442
443
444
445
446
447
448
449
450

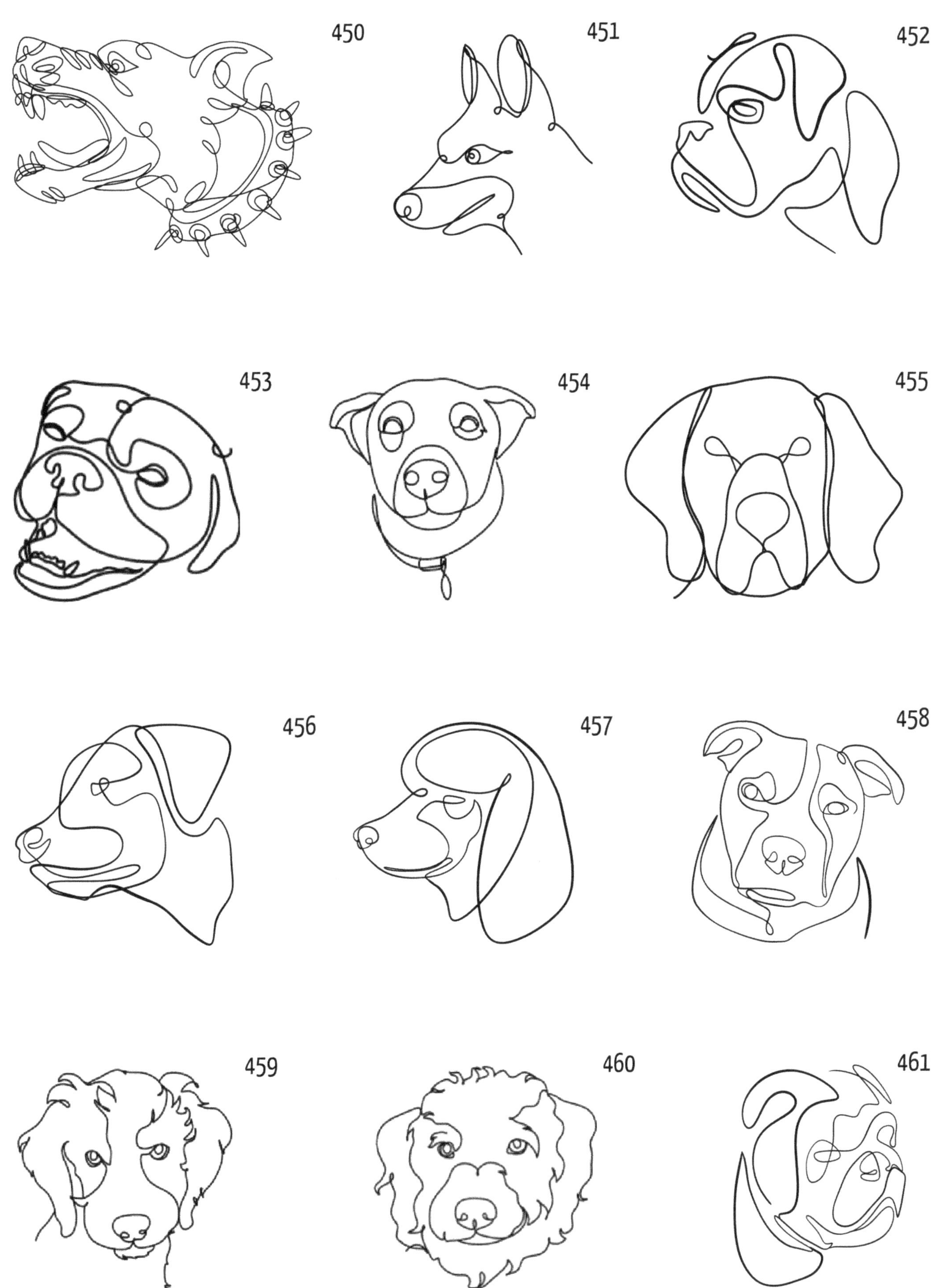

450
451
452
453
454
455
456
457
458
459
460
461

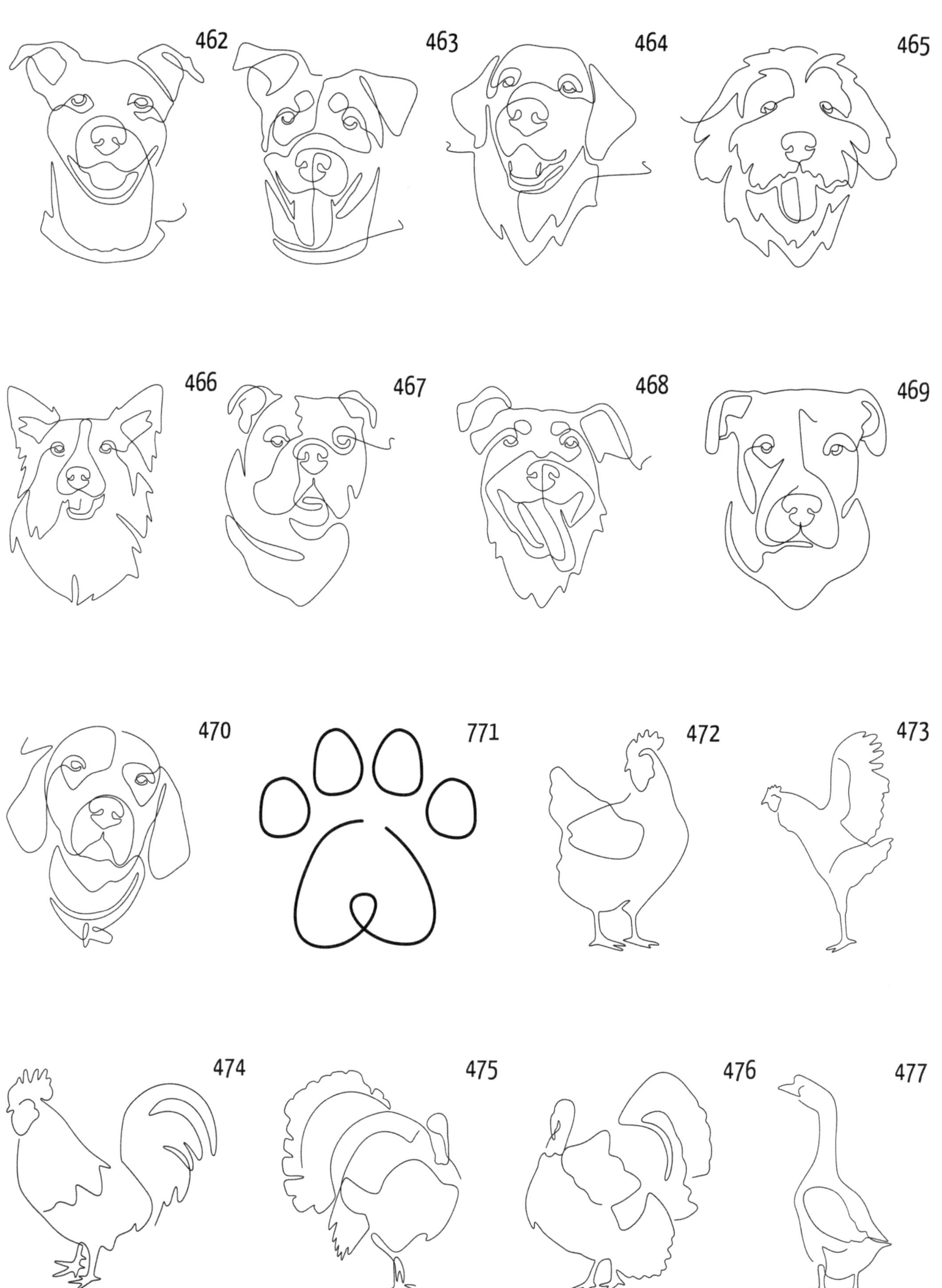

462 463 464 465

466 467 468 469

470 771 472 473

474 475 476 477

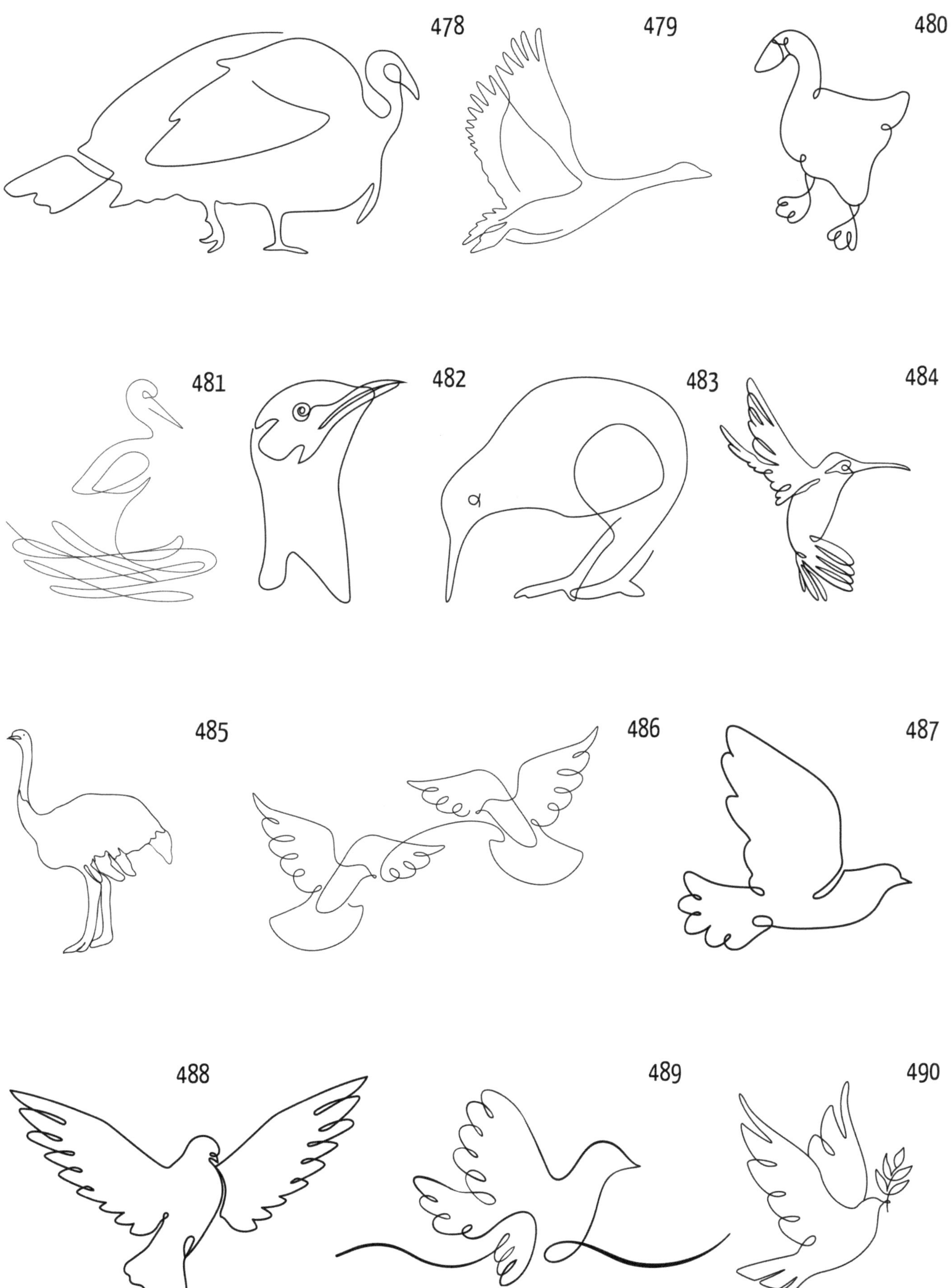
478
479
480
481
482
483
484
485
486
487
488
489
490

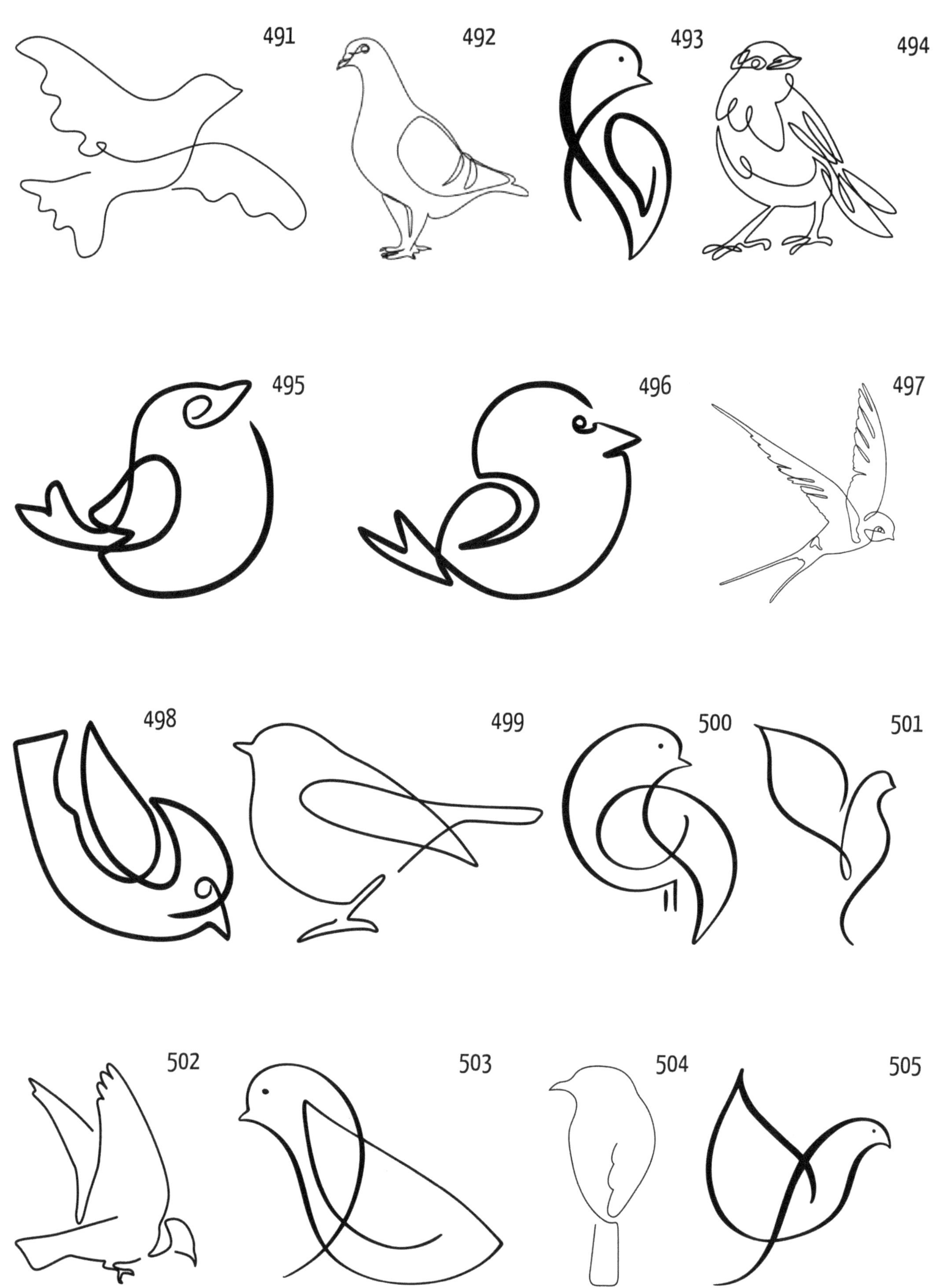
491
492
493
494
495
496
497
498
499
500
501
502
503
504
505

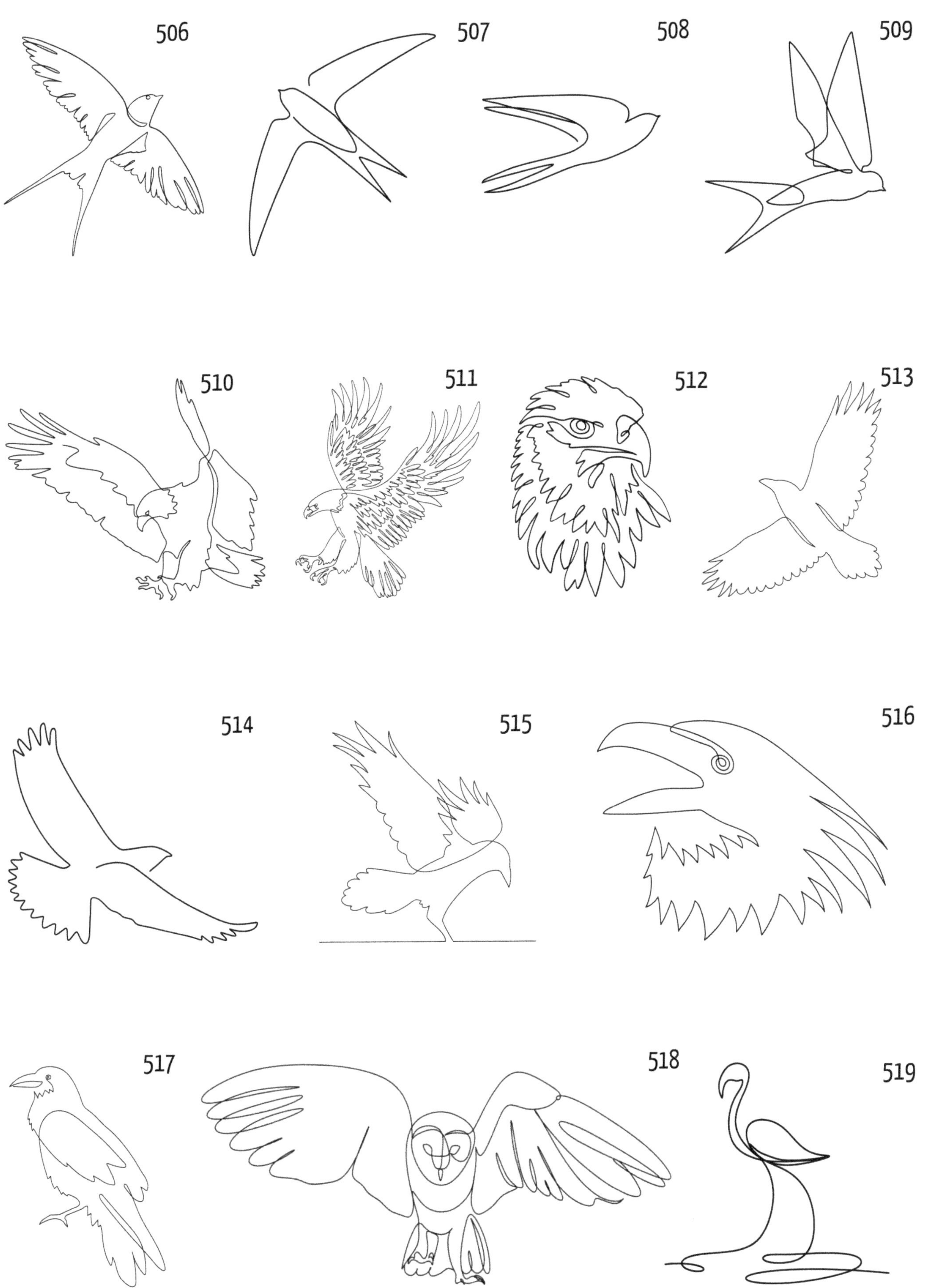

506
507
508
509
510
511
512
513
514
515
516
517
518
519

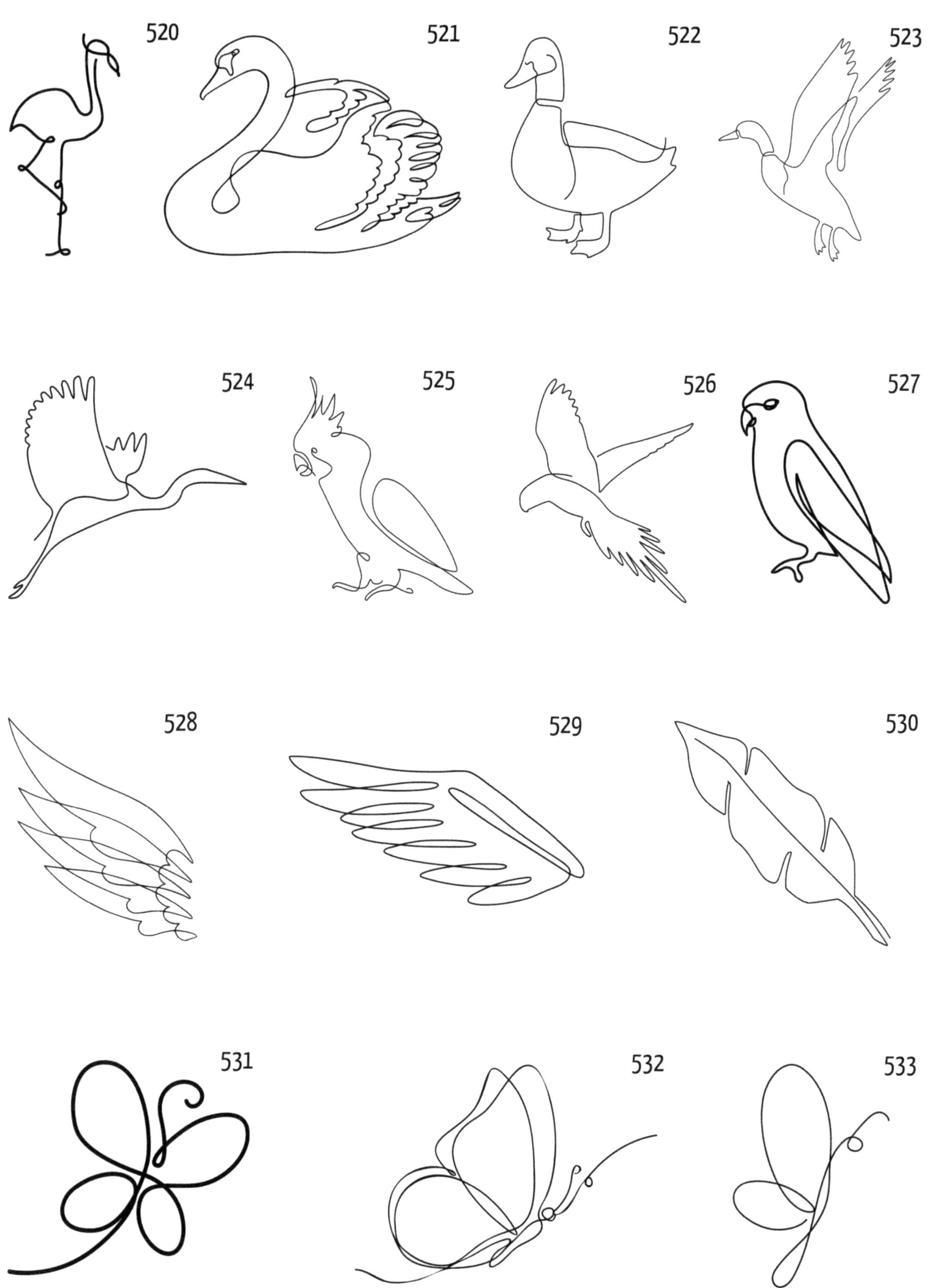

520
521
522
523
524
525
526
527
528
529
530
531
532
533

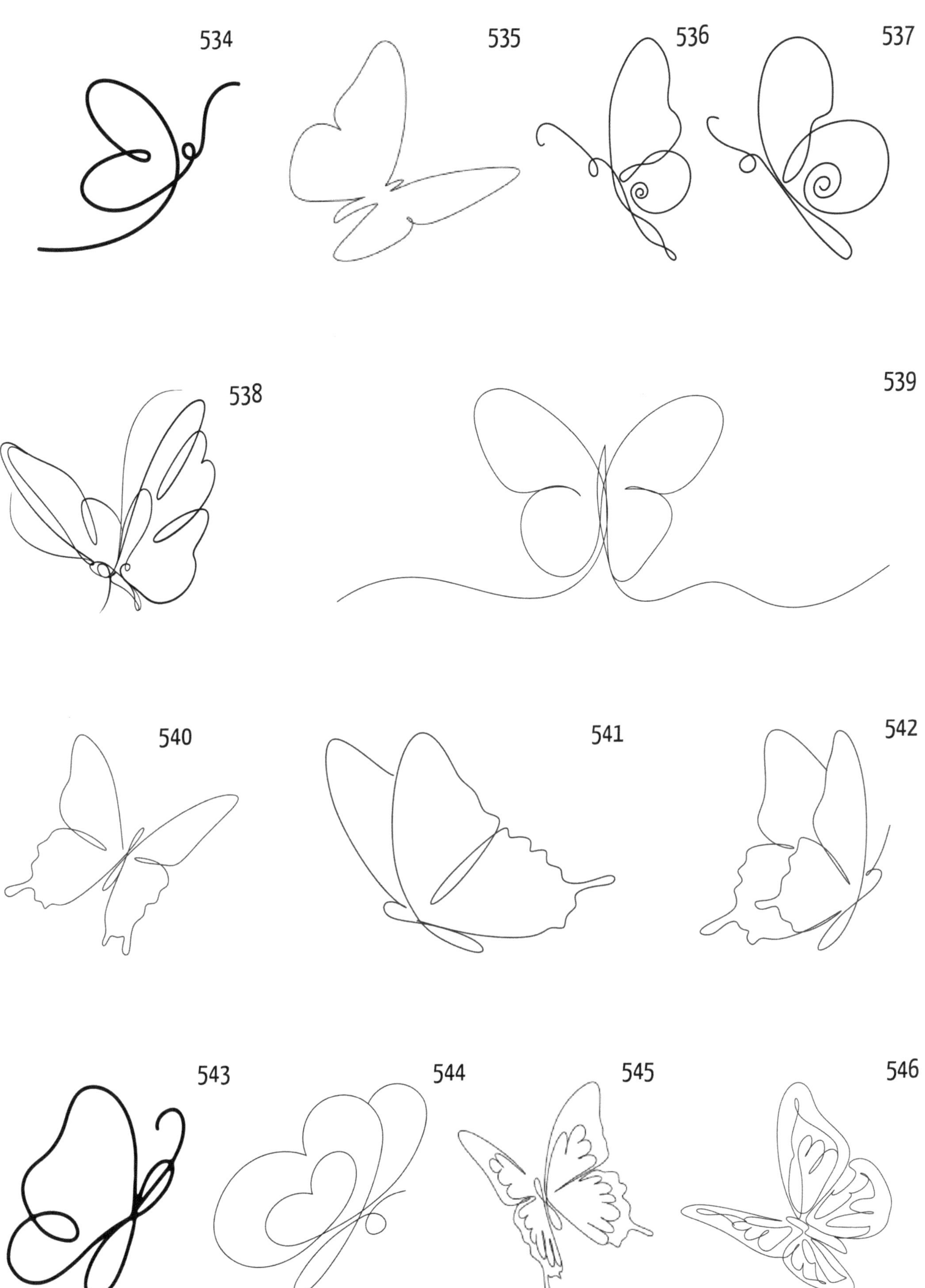

534
535
536
537
538
539
540
541
542
543
544
545
546

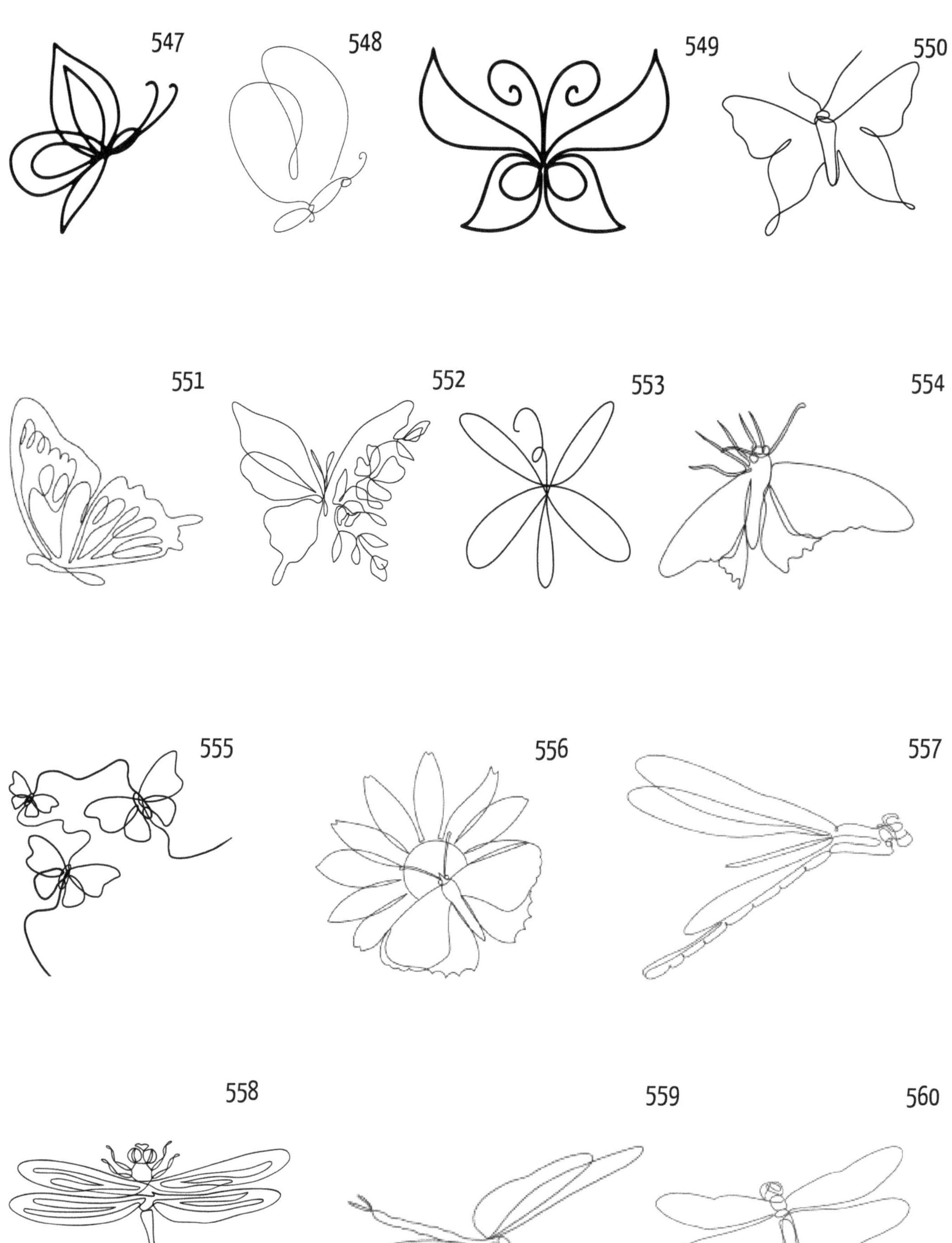

547
548
549
550
551
552
553
554
555
556
557
558
559
560

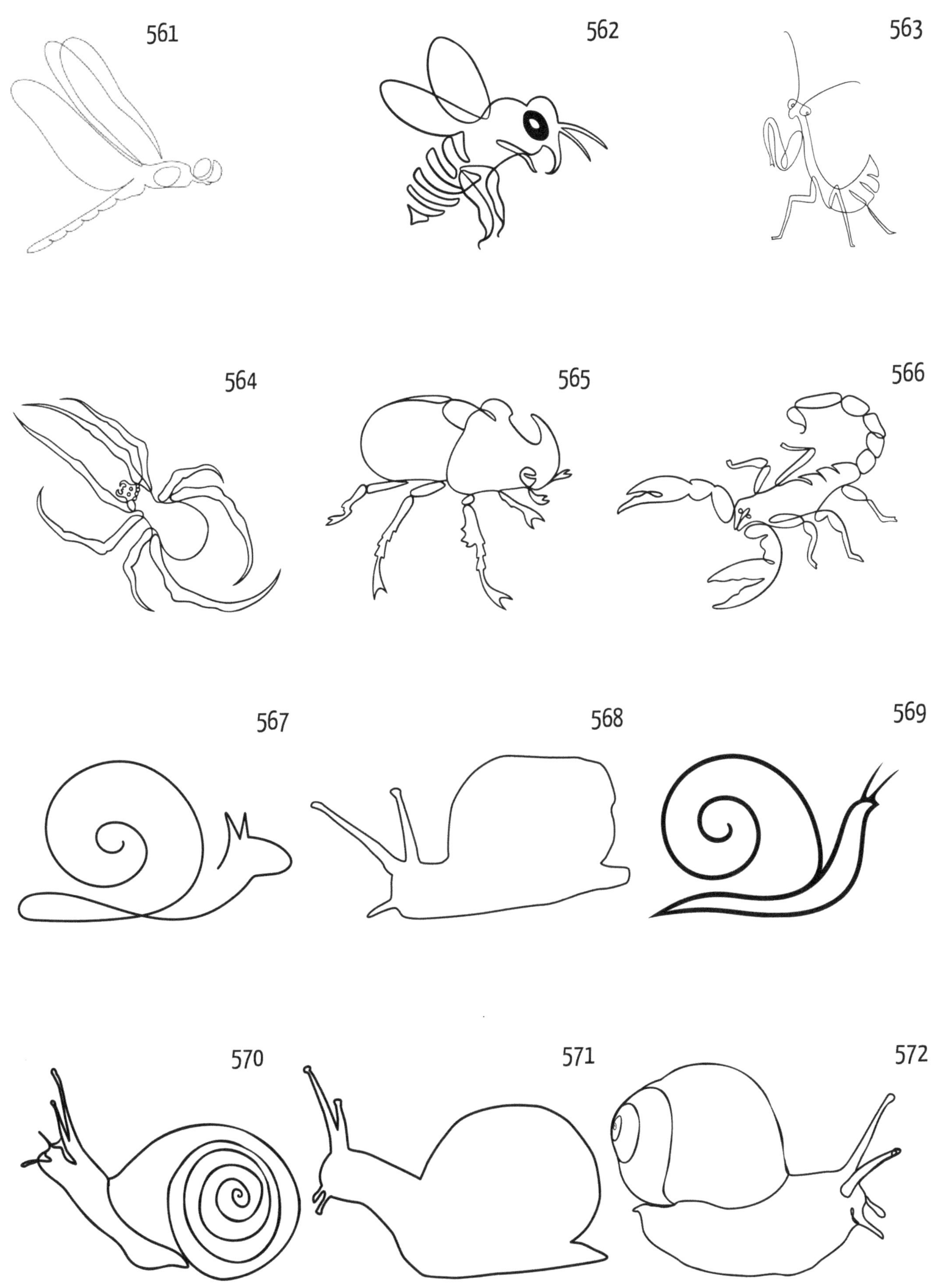

561
562
563
564
565
566
567
568
569
570
571
572

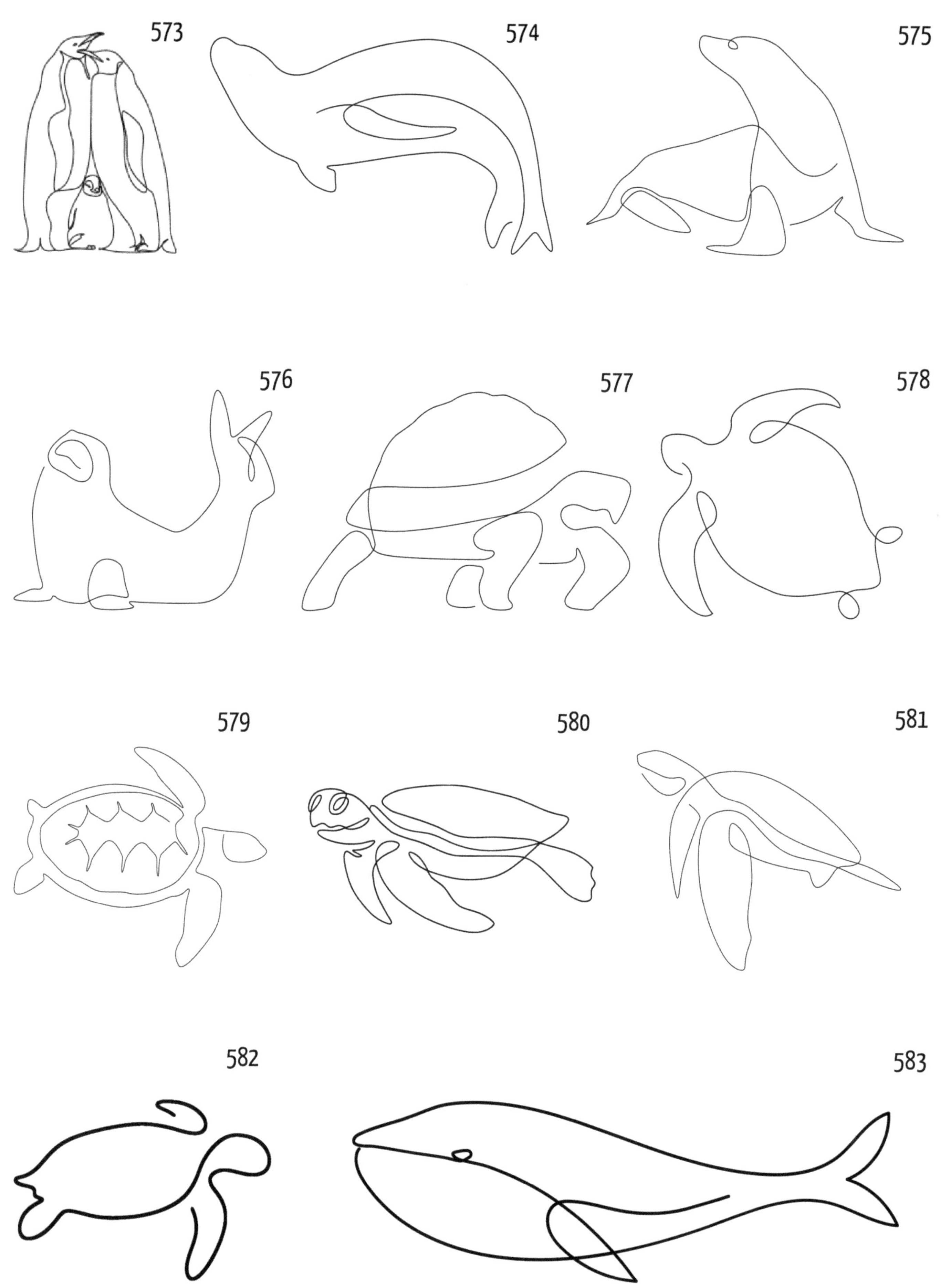

573
574
575
576
577
578
579
580
581
582
583

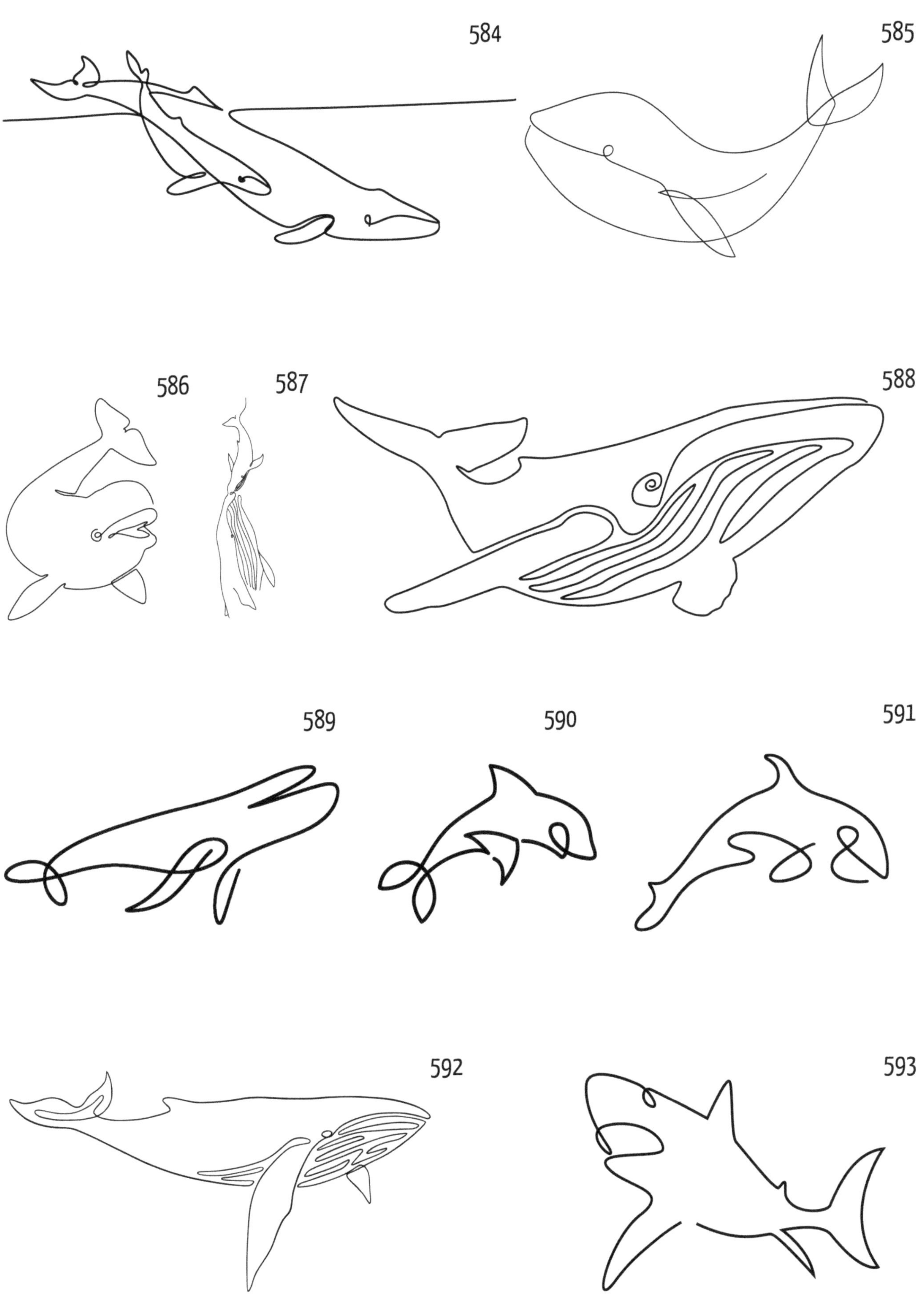
584
585
586
587
588
589
590
591
592
593

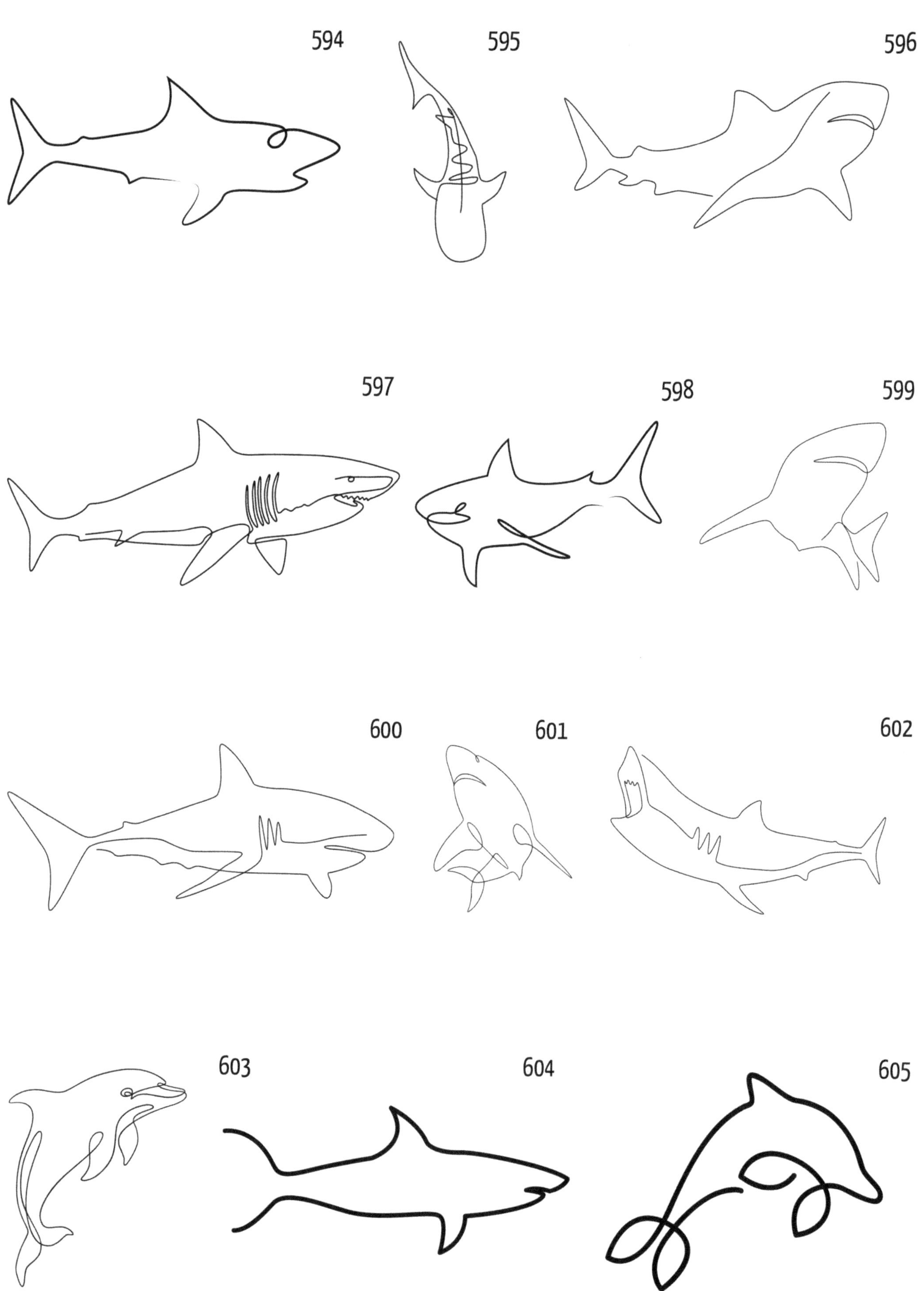

594
595
596
597
598
599
600
601
602
603
604
605

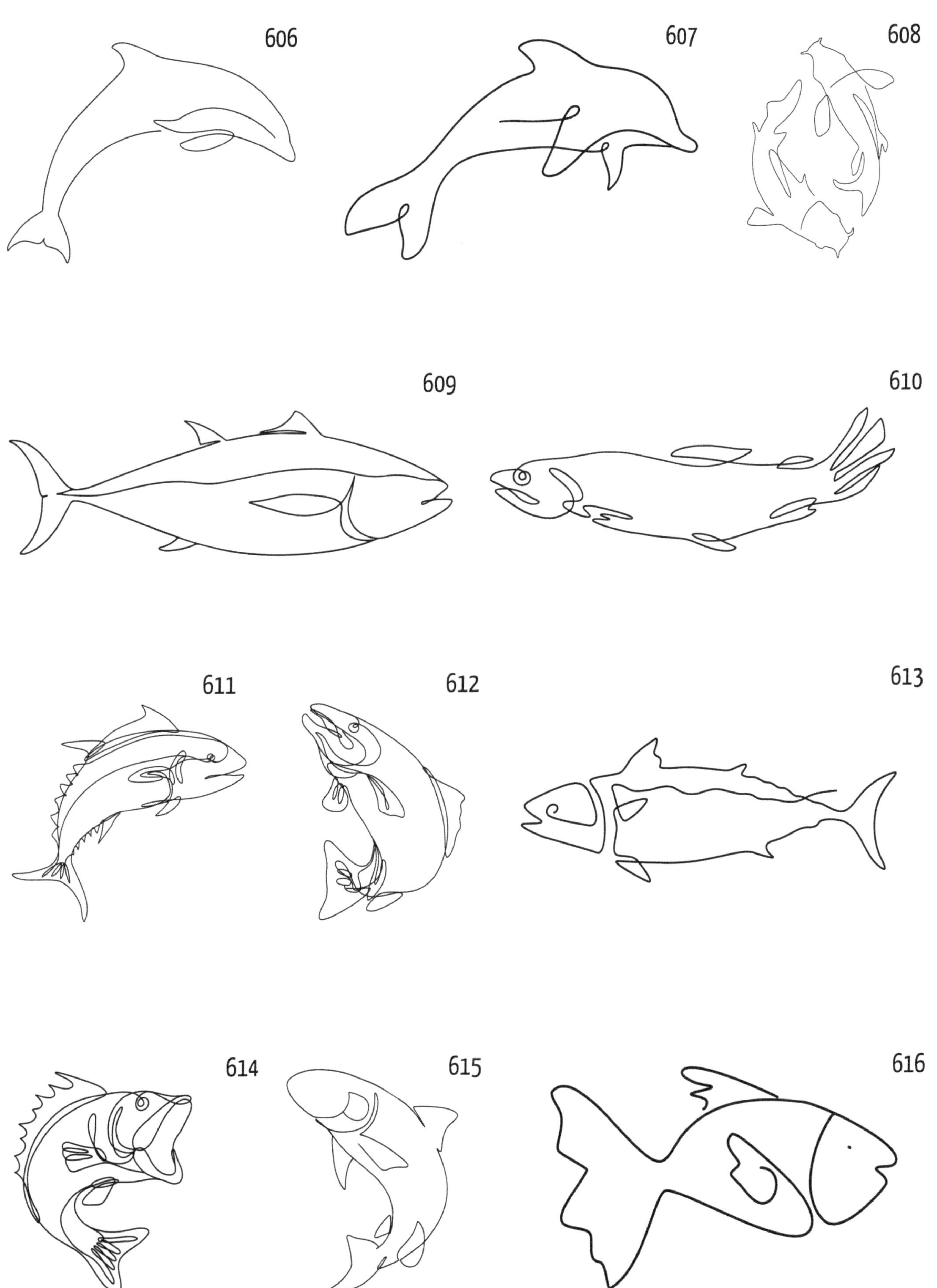

606
607
608
609
610
611
612
613
614
615
616

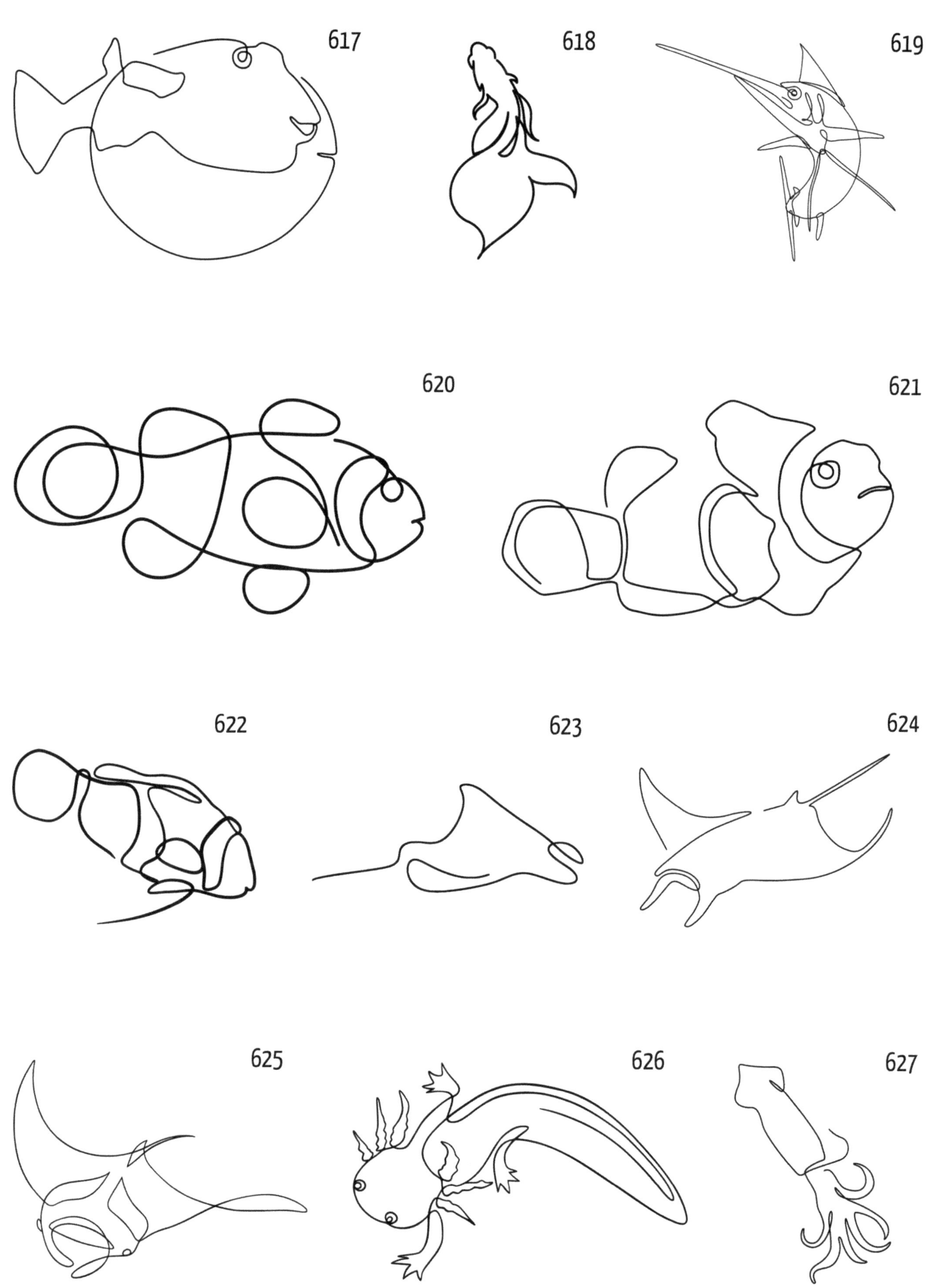

617
618
619
620
621
622
623
624
625
626
627

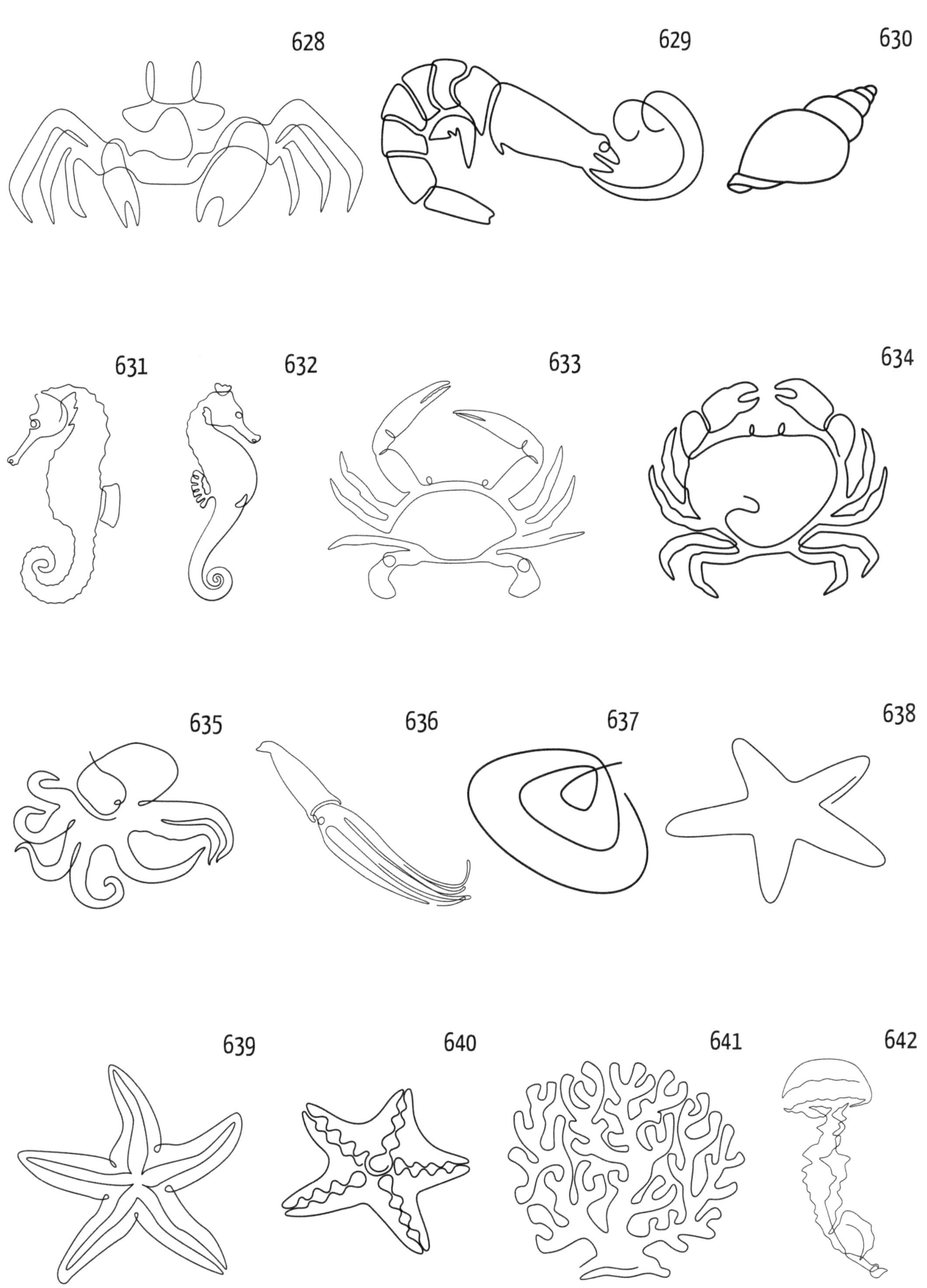

628
629
630
631
632
633
634
635
636
637
638
639
640
641
642

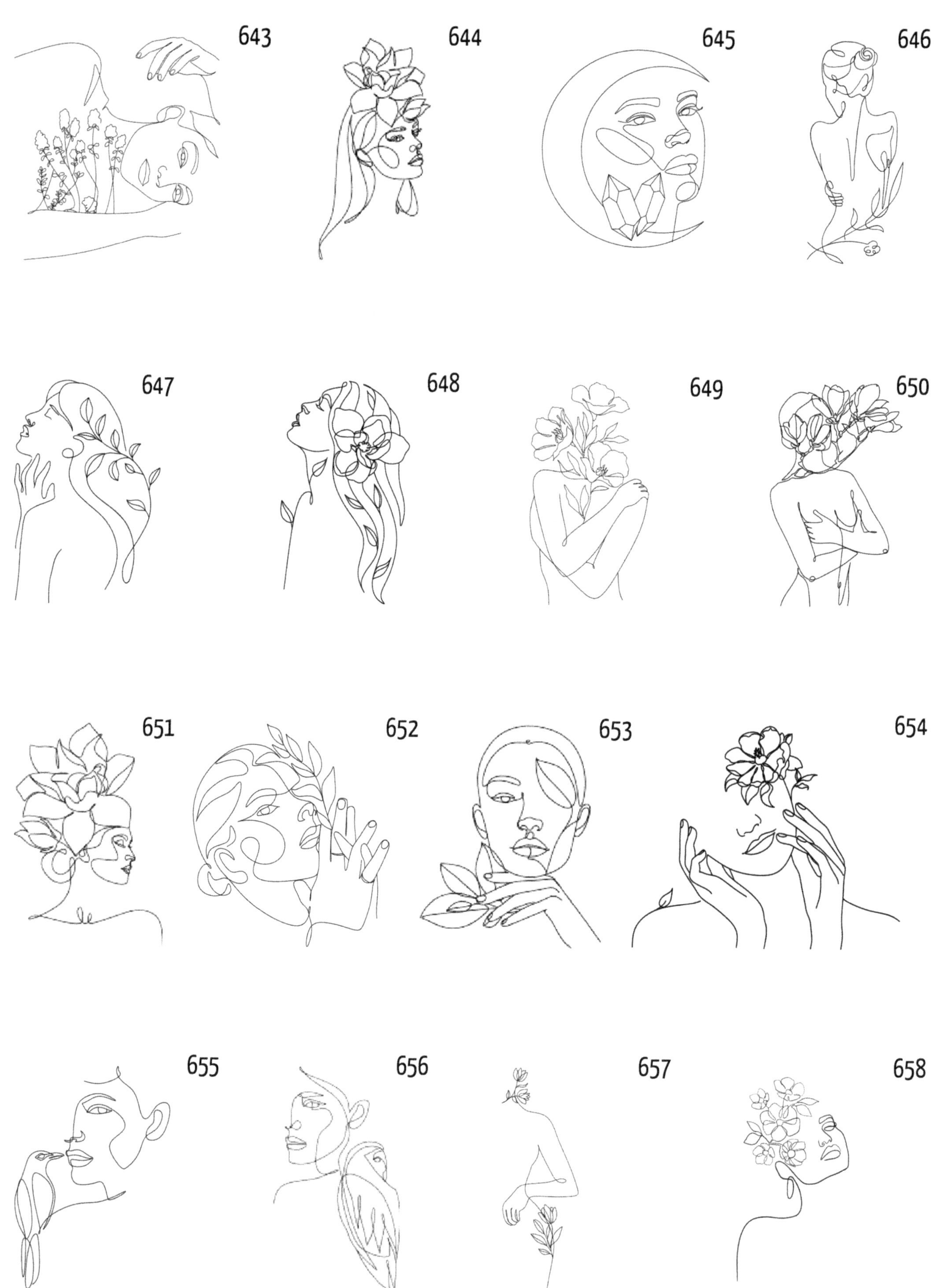

643
644
645
646
647
648
649
650
651
652
653
654
655
656
657
658

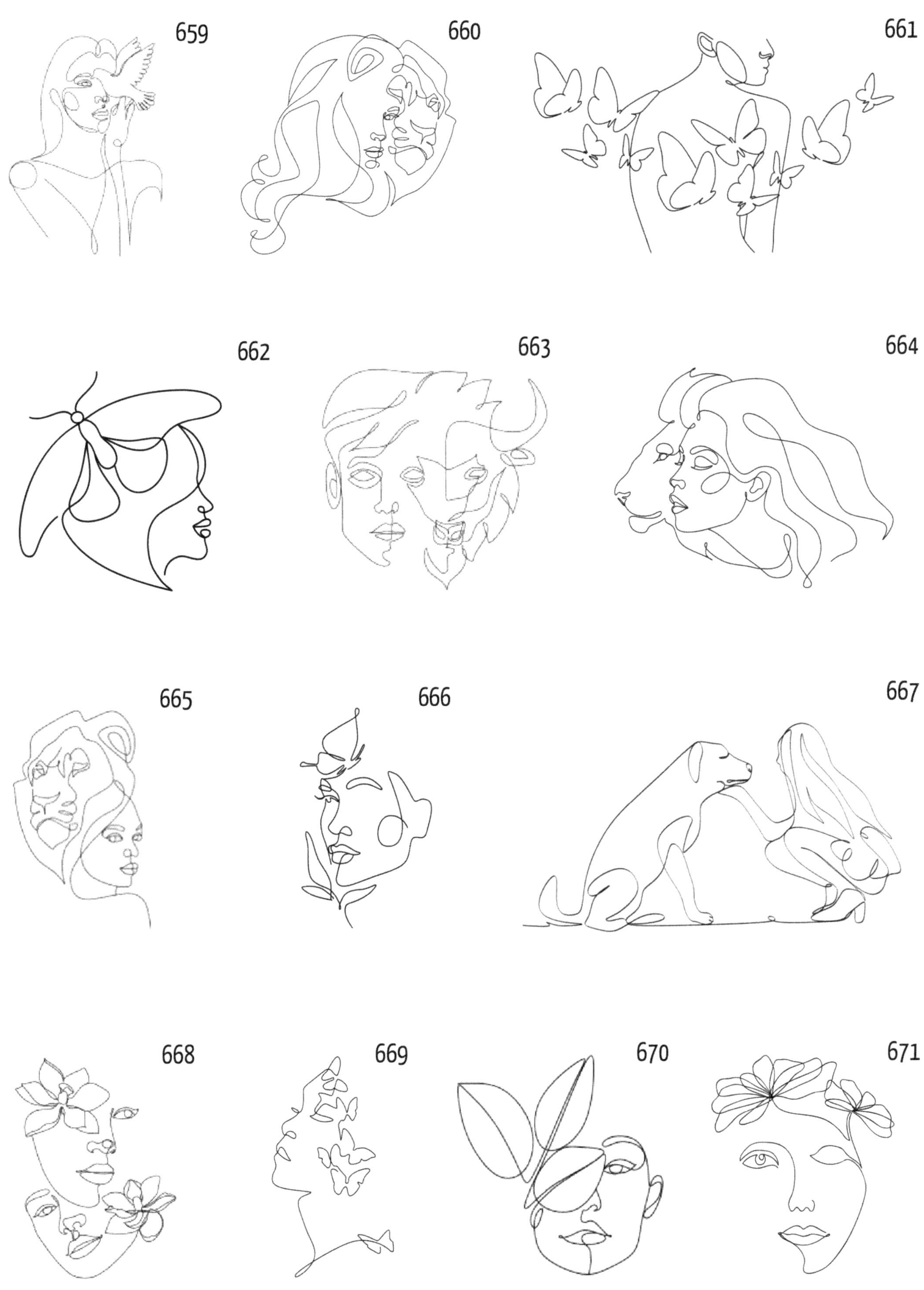

659
660
661
662
663
664
665
666
667
668
669
670
671

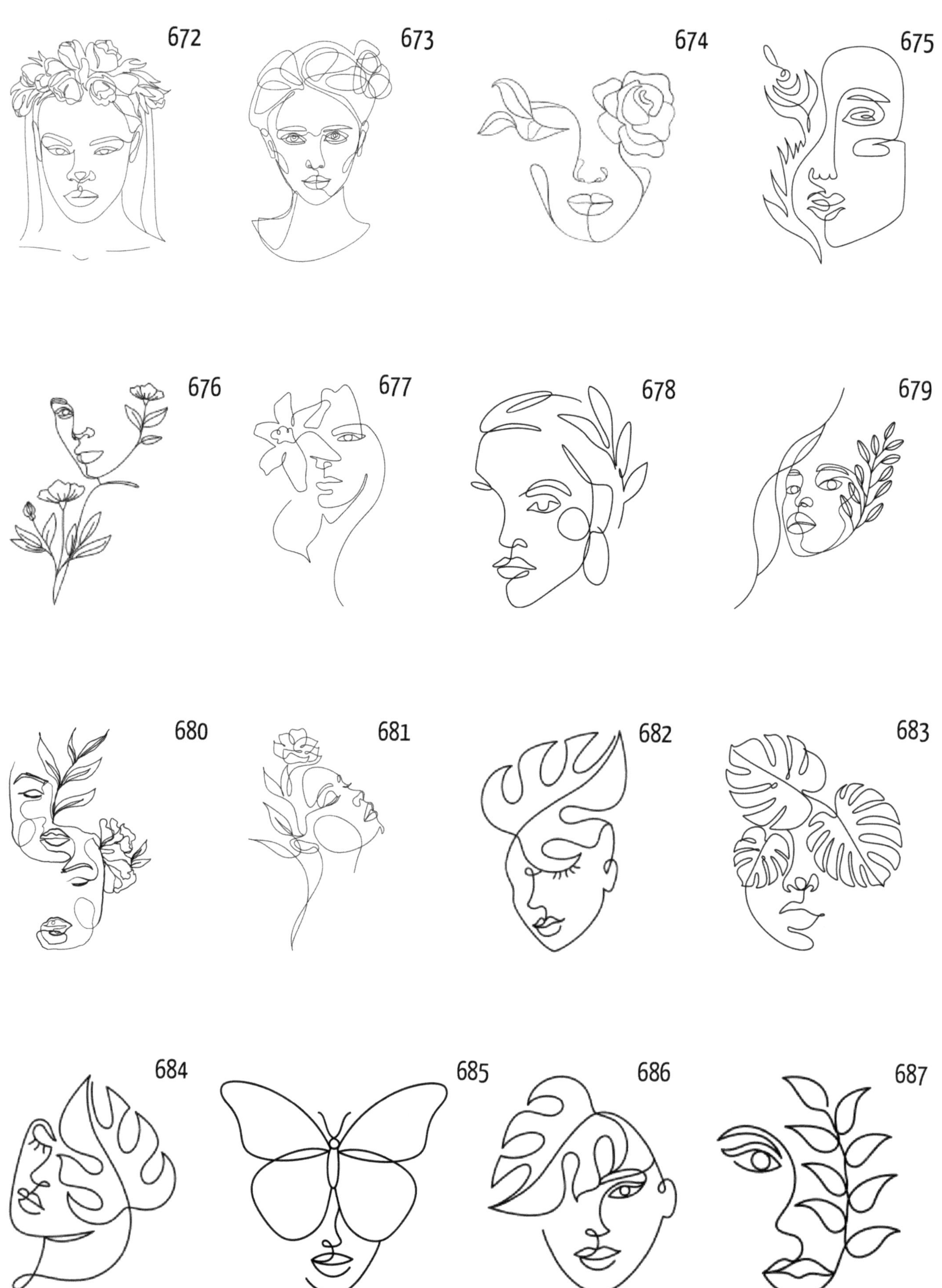

672
673
674
675
676
677
678
679
680
681
682
683
684
685
686
687

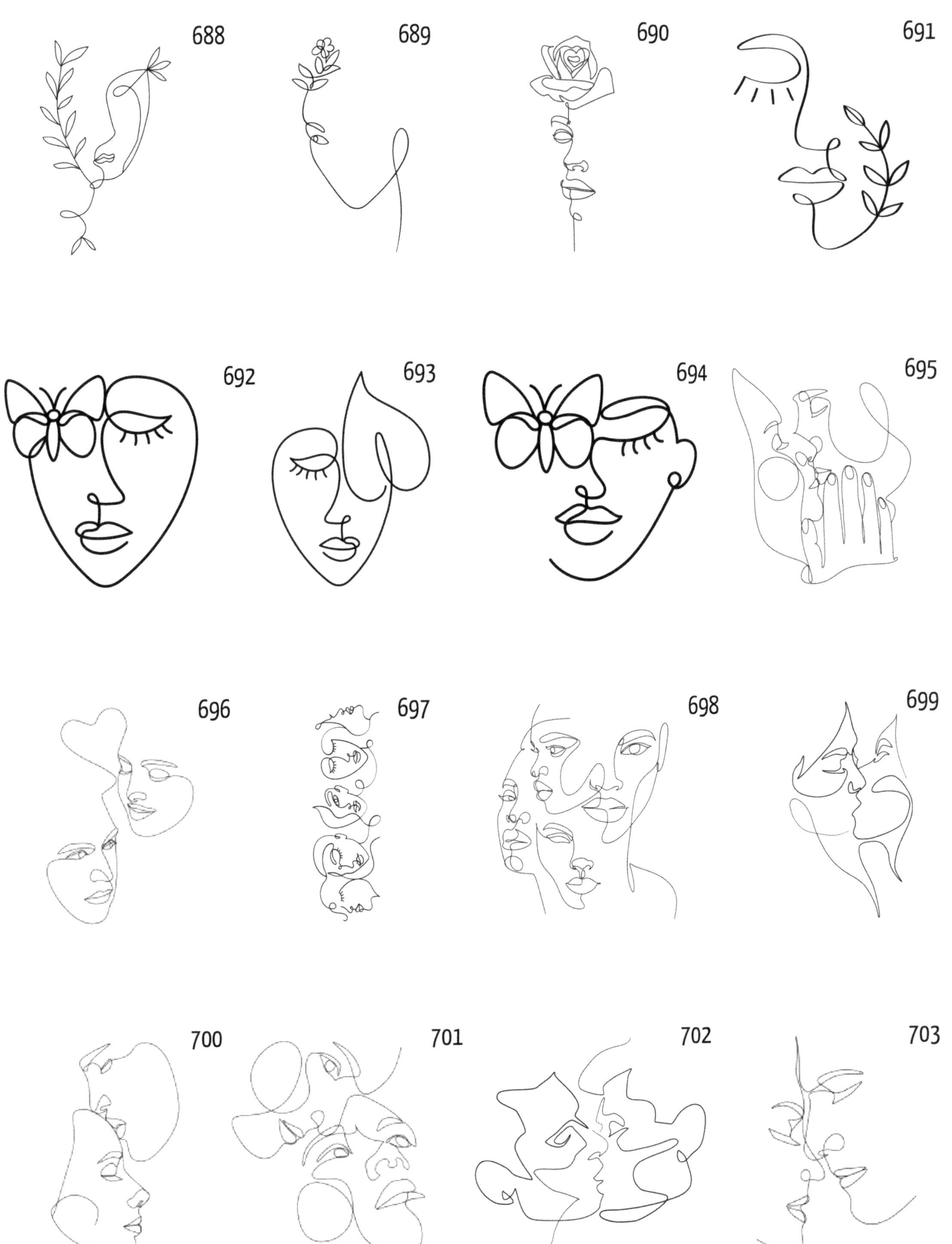

688
689
690
691
692
693
694
695
696
697
698
699
700
701
702
703

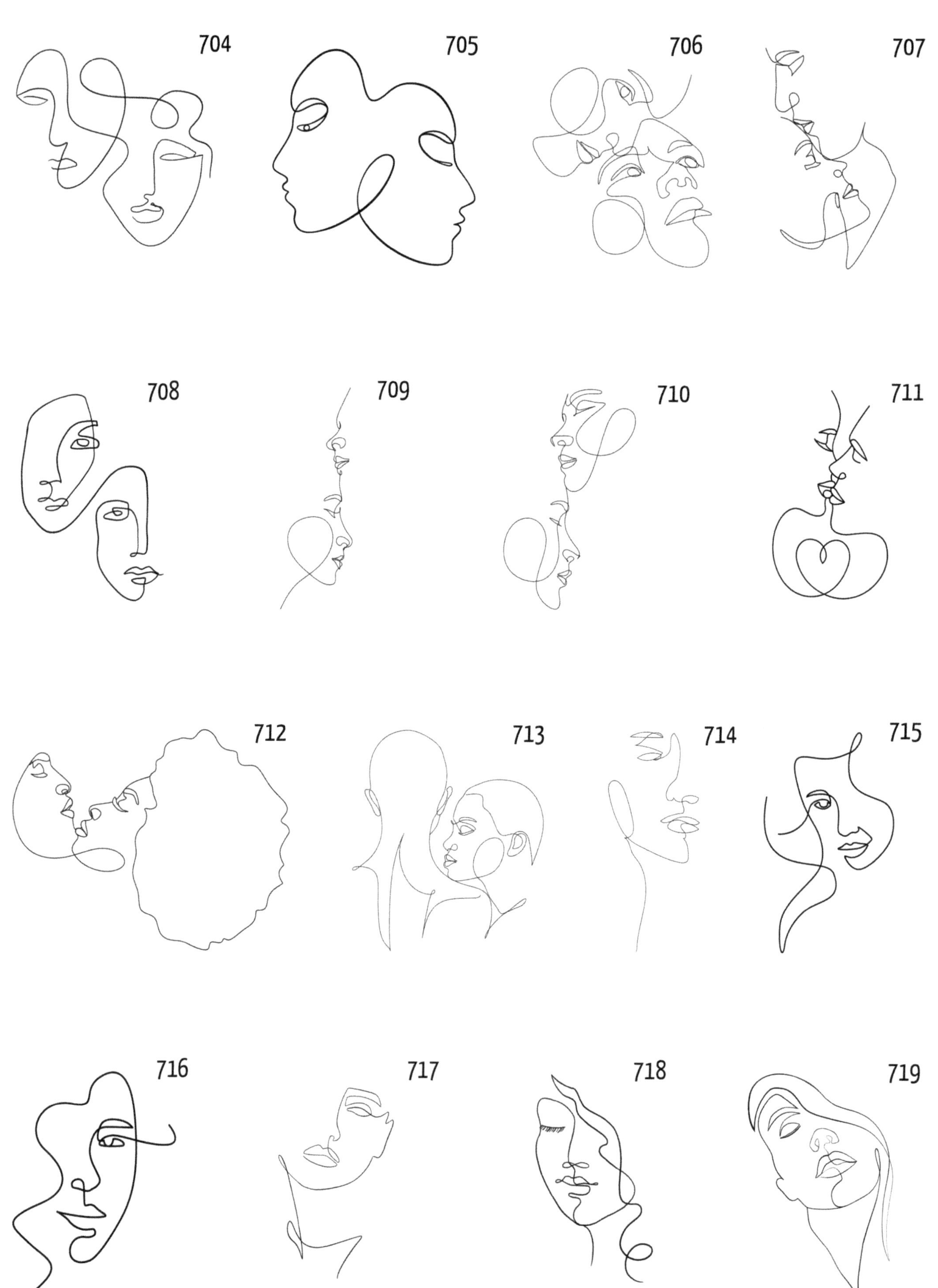

704
705
706
707
708
709
710
711
712
713
714
715
716
717
718
719

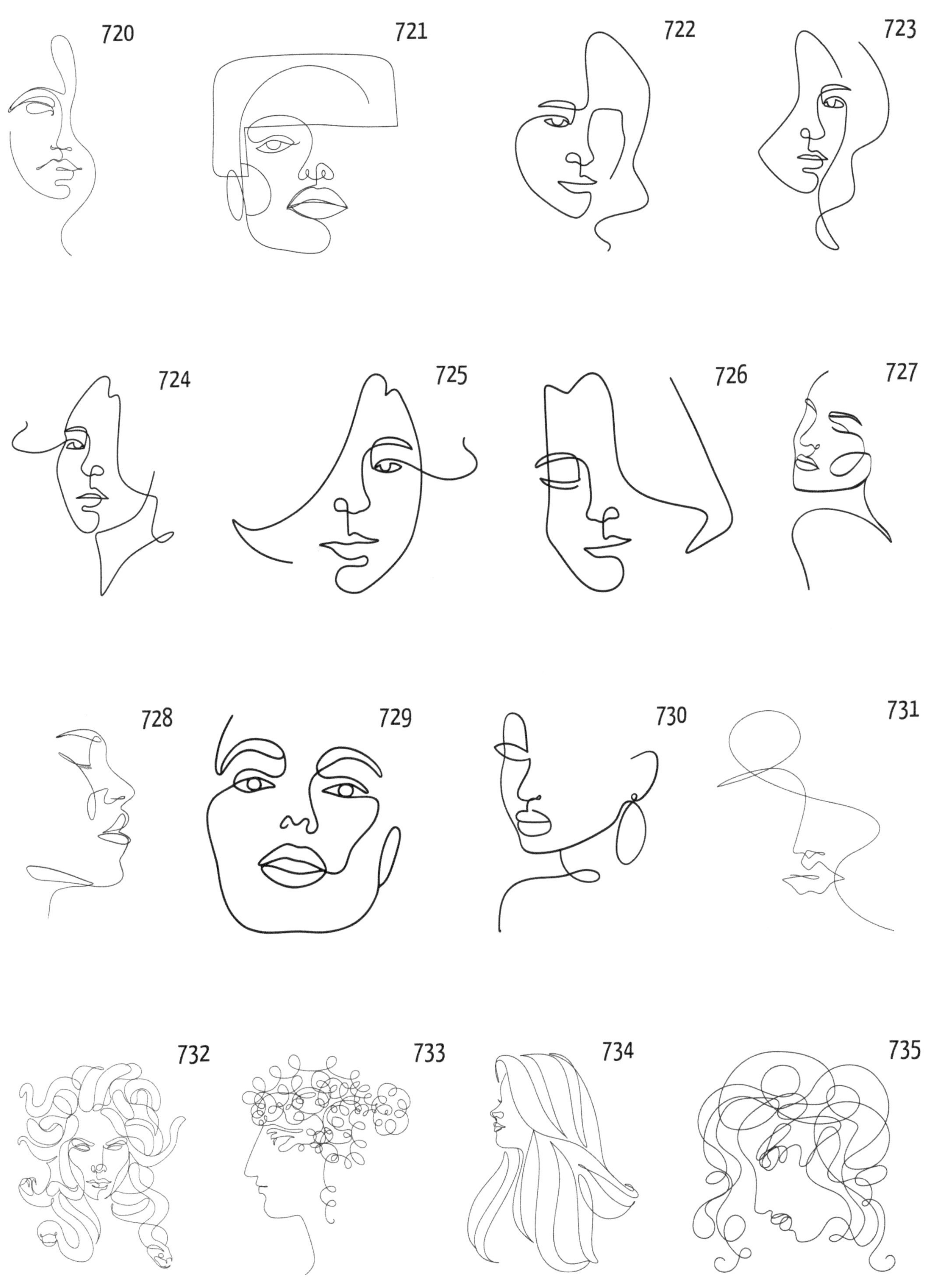

720
721
722
723
724
725
726
727
728
729
730
731
732
733
734
735

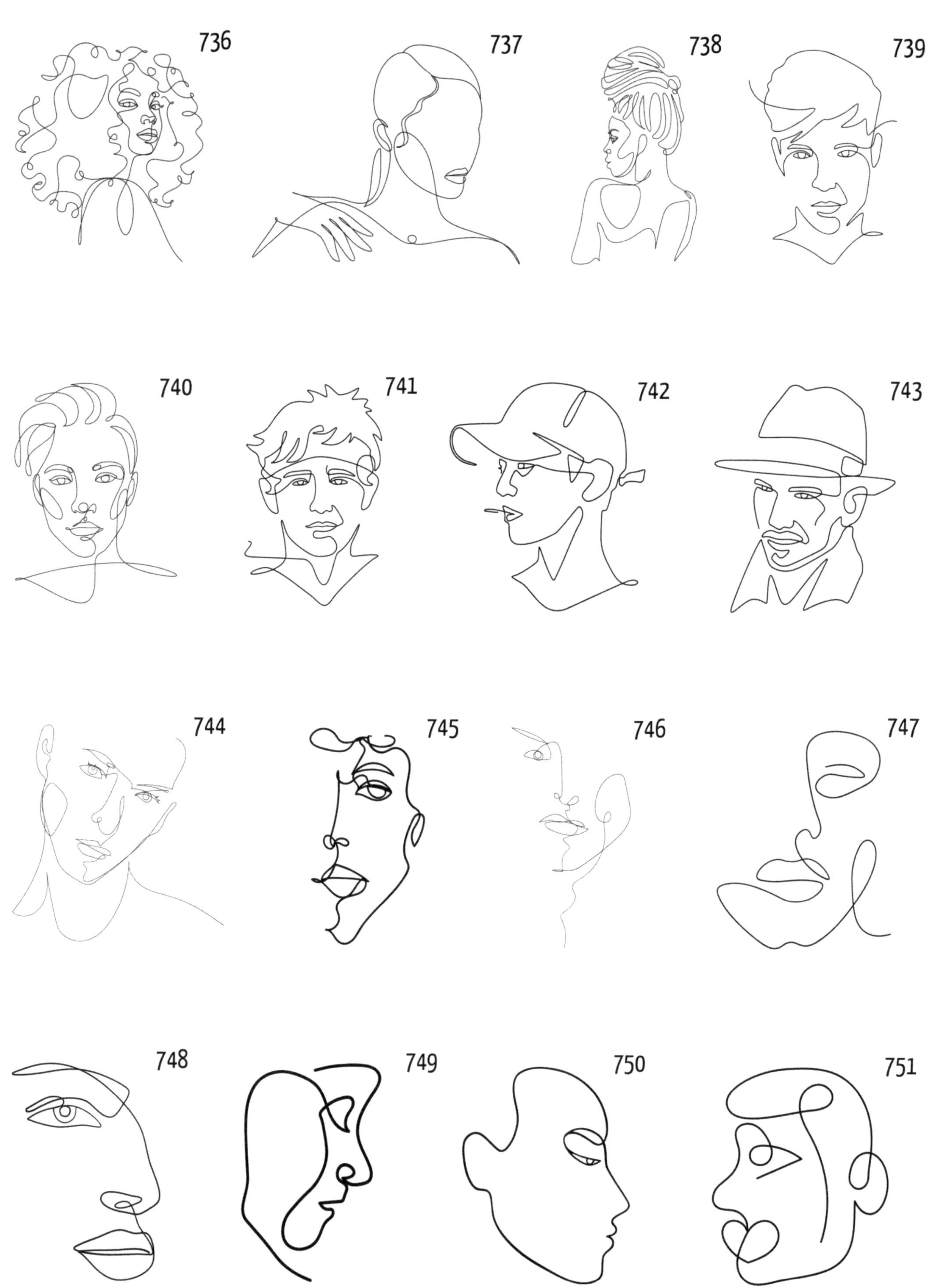

736
737
738
739
740
741
742
743
744
745
746
747
748
749
750
751

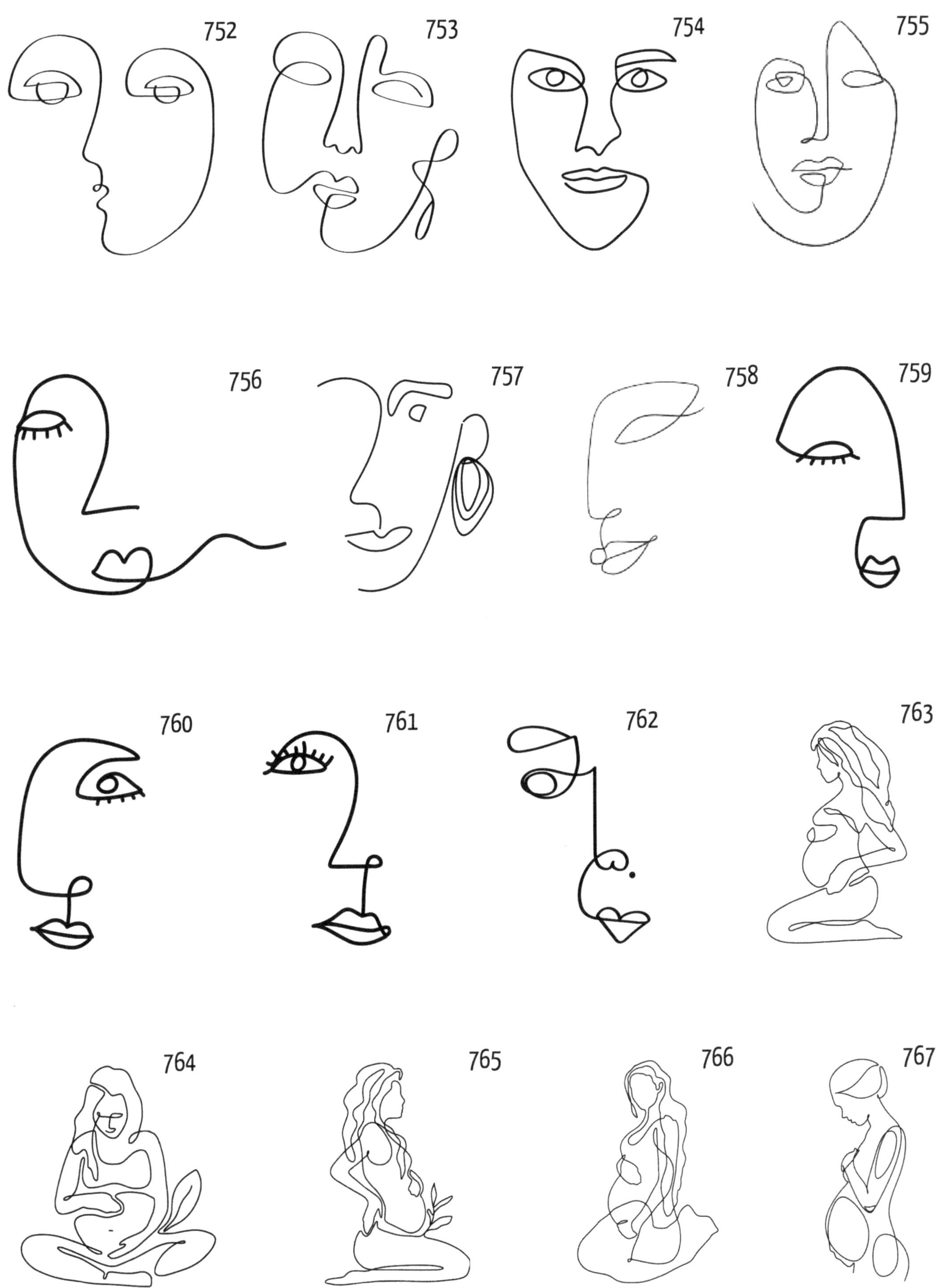

752
753
754
755
756
757
758
759
760
761
762
763
764
765
766
767

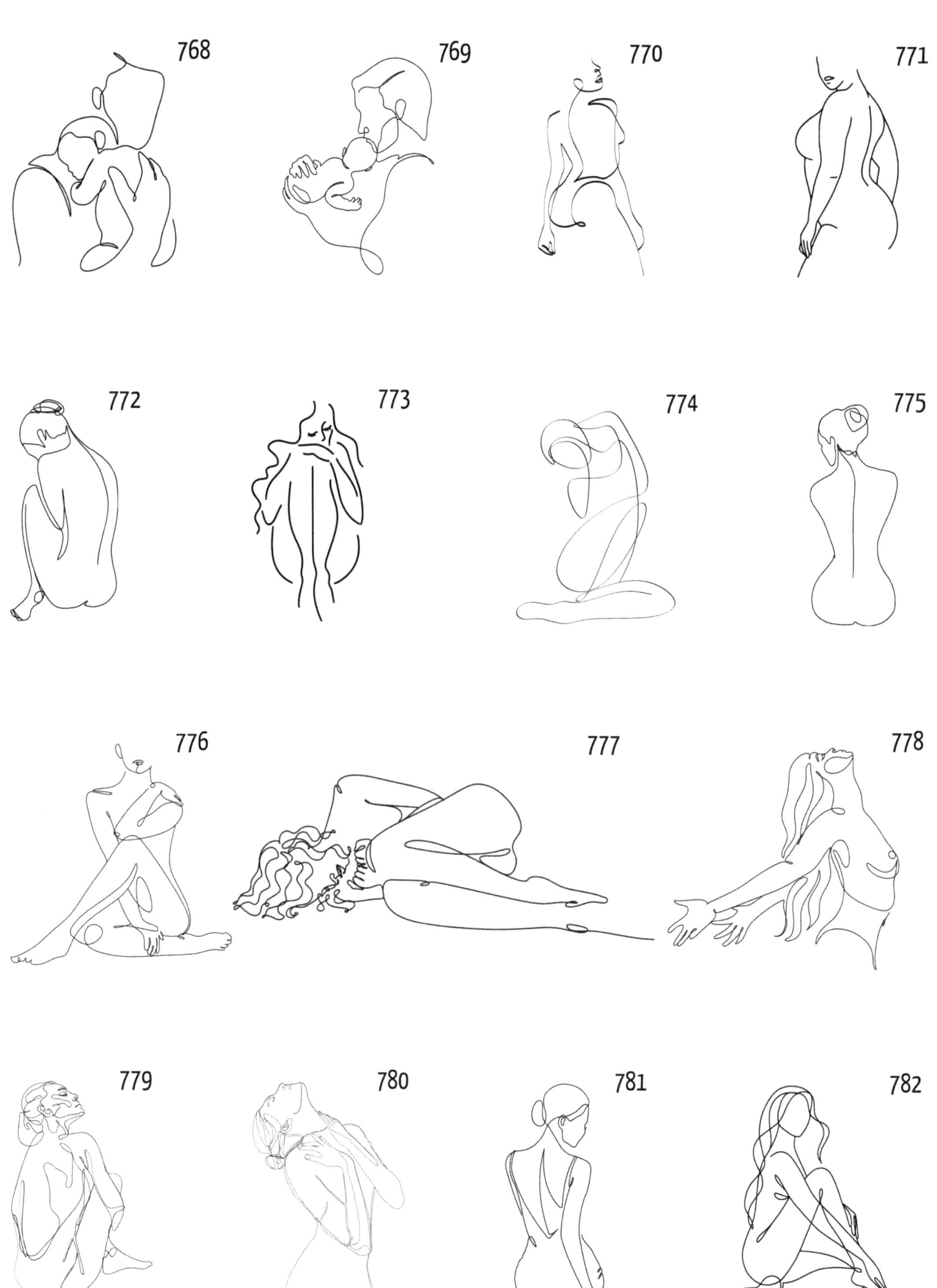
768
769
770
771
772
773
774
775
776
777
778
779
780
781
782

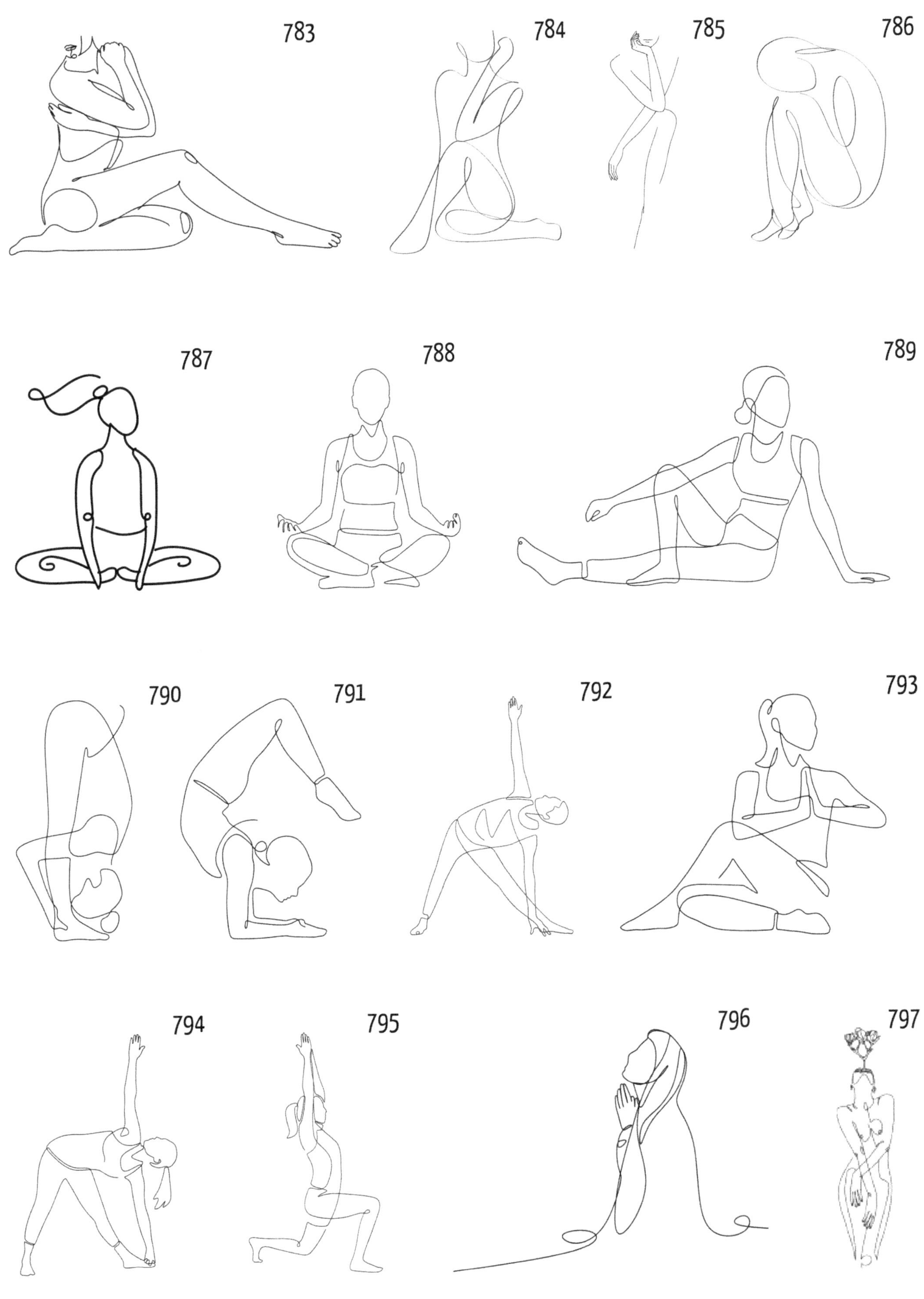

783
784
785
786
787
788
789
790
791
792
793
794
795
796
797

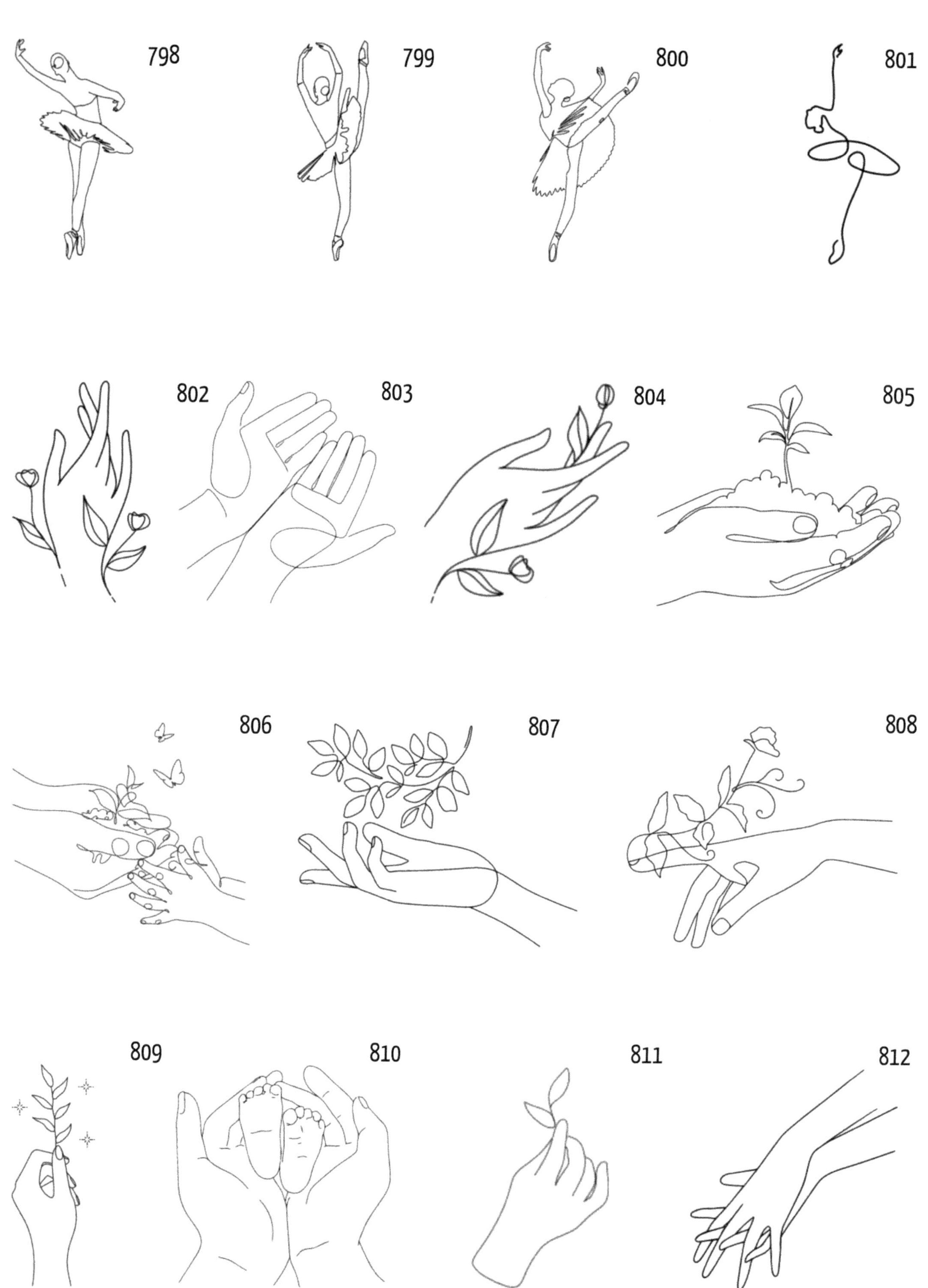

798
799
800
801
802
803
804
805
806
807
808
809
810
811
812

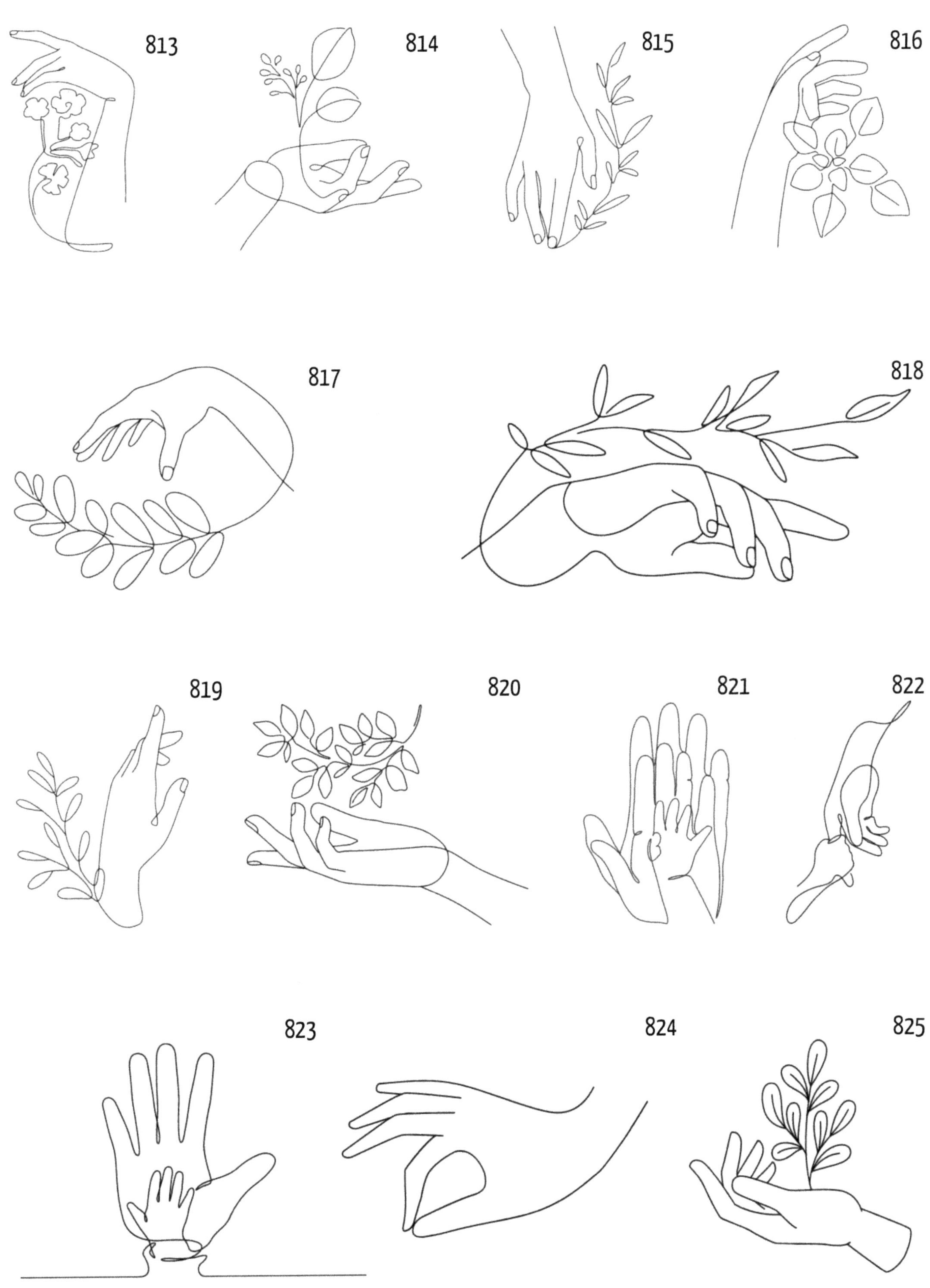

813
814
815
816
817
818
819
820
821
822
823
824
825

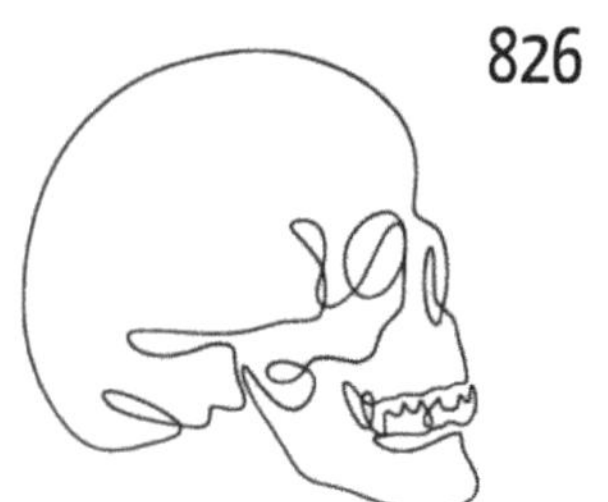 826

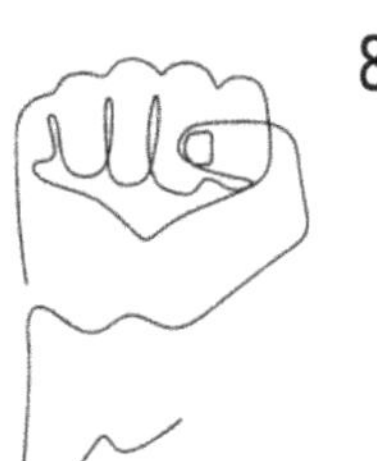 827

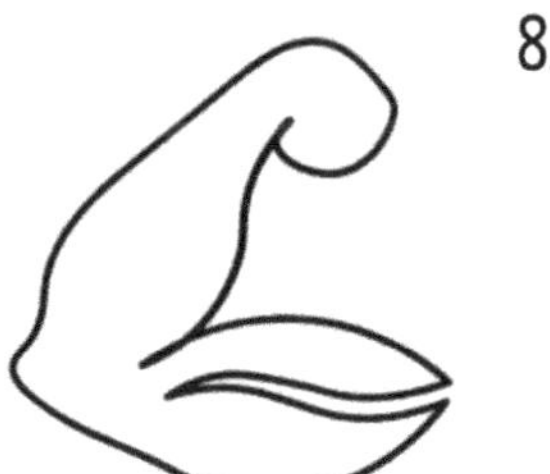 828

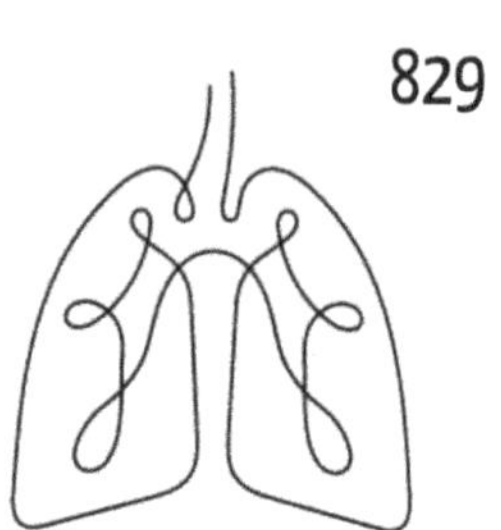 829

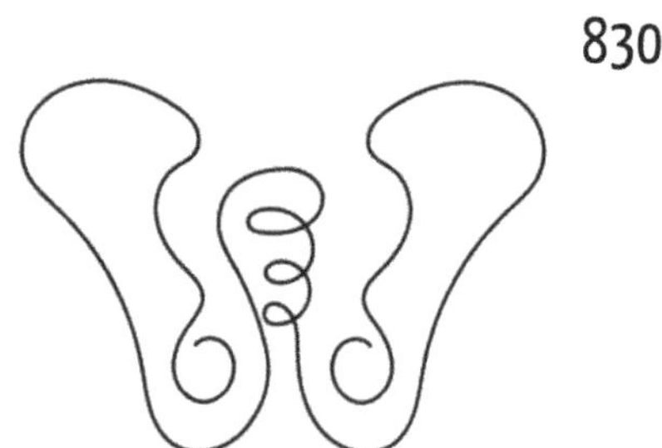 830

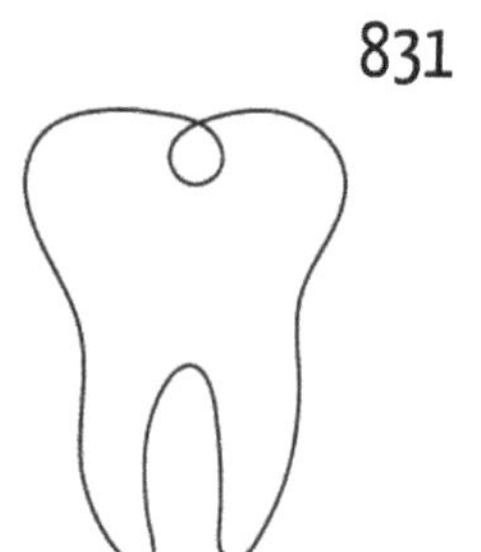 831

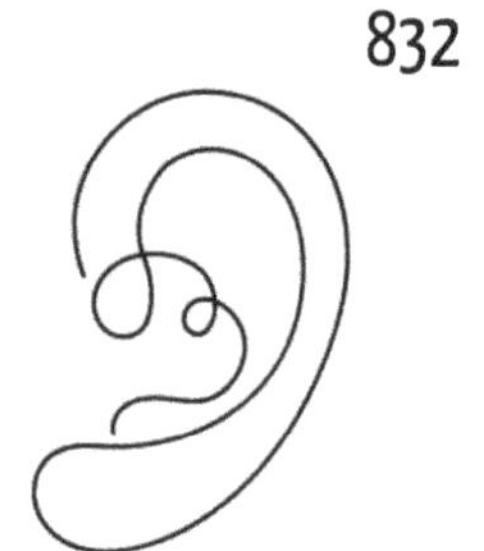 832

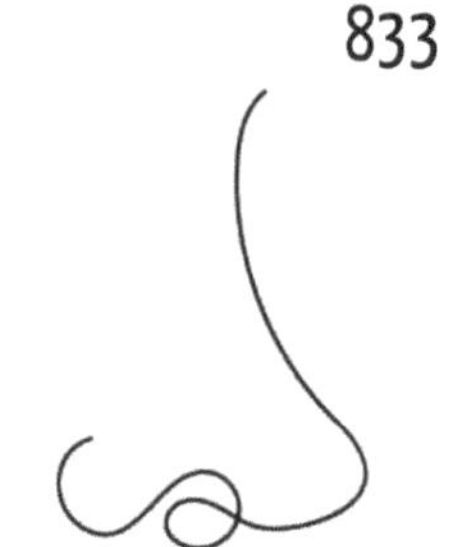 833

834

835

836

837

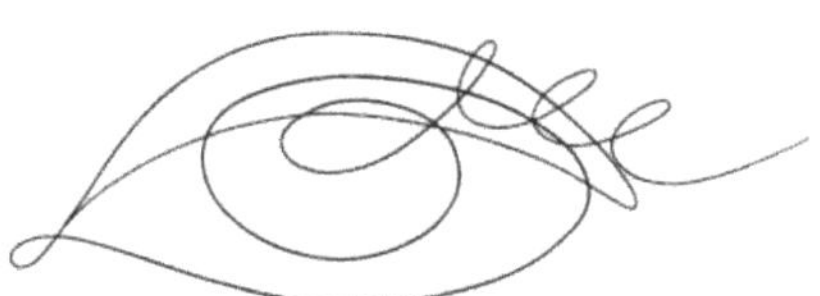

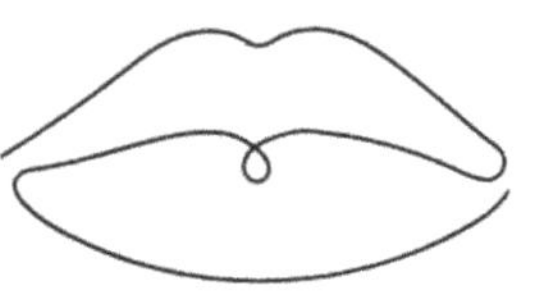

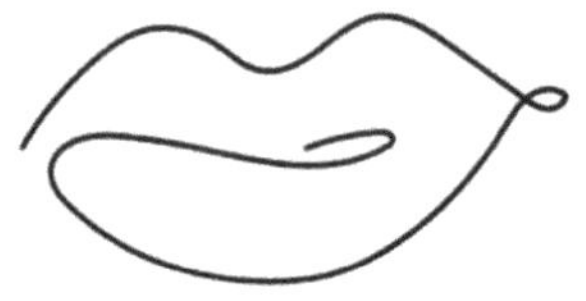

Check these books out:

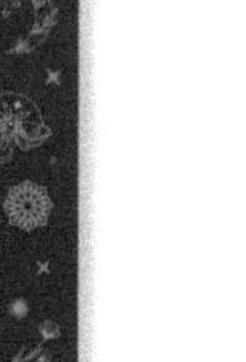

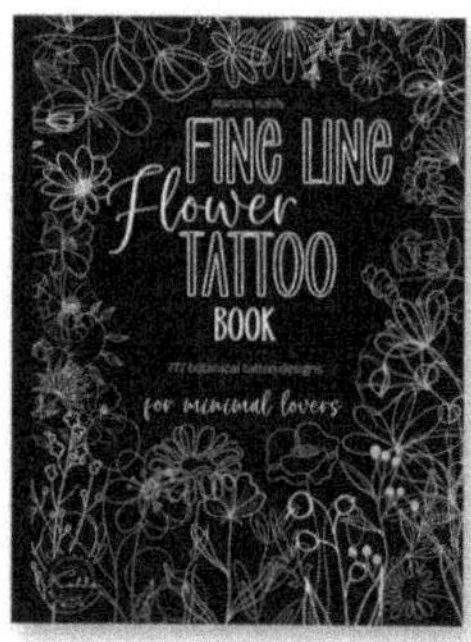

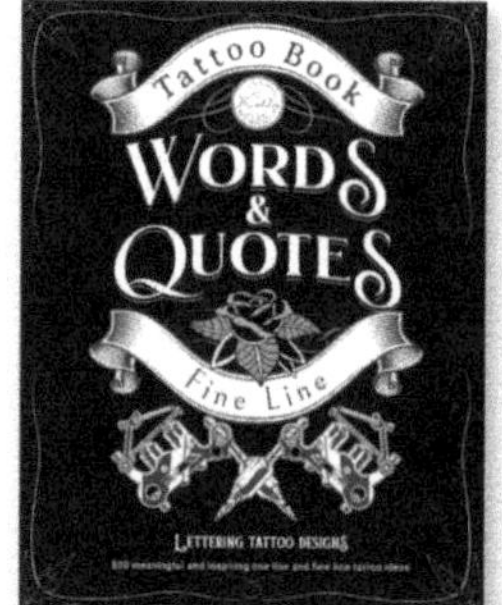

Impressum

Kohls Digiworx
vertreten durch:
Martina Kohls, Lindenstrasse 5, 57648 Bölsberg
Deutschland
ISBN: 978-3-910363-04-5
Independently Published
This book was printed by IngramSpark©